The City in Biblical Perspective

Biblical Challenges in the Contemporary World

Editor: J. W. Rogerson, University of Sheffield

Current uses of the Bible in debates about issues such as human sexuality, war and wealth and poverty often amount to either a literalist concentration on a few selected texts, or an accommodation of the Bible to secular trends. The "Biblical Challenges" series aims to acquaint readers with the biblical material pertinent to particular issues, including that which causes difficulty or embarrassment in today's world, together with suggestions about how the Bible can nonetheless present a challenge in the contemporary age. The series seeks to open up a critical dialogue between the Bible and the chosen issue, which will lead to a dialogue between the biblical text and readers, challenging them to reflection and praxis. Each volume is designed with the needs of undergraduate and college students in mind, and can serve as a course book either for a complete unit or a component.

Published:

According to the Scriptures?
The Challenge of Using the Bible in Social, Moral and Political Questions
J. W. Rogerson

Forthcoming:

Fundamentalism and the Bible
Harriet A. Harris

Science and Miracle, Faith and Doubt:
A Scientific Theology of the Bible
Mark Harris

The City in Biblical Perspective

J. W. Rogerson and John Vincent

LONDON   OAKVILLE

Published by

UK: Equinox Publishing Ltd., Unit 6, The Village, 101 Amies St., London SW11 2JW
USA: DBBC, 28 Main Street, Oakville, CT 06779

www.equinoxpub.com

First published 2009

British Library Cataloguing-in-Publication Data

A catalogue record for this book is available from the British Library.

ISBN-13   978 184553 289 5   (hardback)
           978 184553 290 1   (paperback)

Library of Congress Cataloging-in-Publication Data

Rogerson, J. W. (John William), 1935-
  The city in biblical perspective / J.W. Rogerson and John J. Vincent.
     p. cm. — (Biblical challenges in the contemporary world)
  Includes bibliographical references and index.
  ISBN 978-1-84553-289-5 (hb)
  ISBN 978-1-84553-290-1 (pbk.) 1.
Cities and towns—Biblical teaching. I. Vincent, John J. II. Title.
  BR115.C45R64 2009
  220.8'30776—dc22

                              2008039136

Typeset by S.J.I. Services, New Delhi
Printed and bound in Great Britain by Lightning Source (UK) Ltd, Milton Keynes

CONTENTS

From time to time the need to write about specific topics reveals how different the Old Testament can be from the New. Many years ago when I was working on an *Atlas of the Bible* I was struck by the fact that whereas Galilee was of little importance in the Old Testament it was central in the New, being the main location of the ministry of Jesus. The reason for this difference was that Galilee had been lost by the Northern Kingdom, Israel, in the ninth century BCE and had only been regained by Judah around a century before the birth of Jesus. The difference between the two Testaments is also striking when it comes to the subject of the city. Israelite cities were small: smaller than the Canaanite cities on whose sites they had sometimes been rebuilt, and much smaller than the great cities of empire such as Nineveh or Mari. Even the Jerusalem of Old Testament times was considerably smaller than that of the New Testament era, where the technology of bringing water to the city by means of aqueducts had enabled its population to expand on the hills to the west and north of the spur that had accommodated the city of David. Another difference between the Testaments is that the capital cities surrounding the nations of Israel and Judah were experienced as threats from which invasions took place and to which kings and nobles might be exiled. In the New Testament the spread of the Roman Empire meant that cities such as Antioch, Corinth and even Rome itself were places where Christian communities had been established and where Christian discipleship was put into practice.

These differences have affected the treatment of the city in the Old and New Testaments in the present work. But another difference needs to be mentioned. While the Old Testament has much to offer readers today by way of reflection on the city as a centre of power or of aggression, or even as a target in times of war, it does not engage Christian readers in the same way as the New Testament. Because Christian discipleship involves taking seriously the life and teaching of Jesus and the first Christians, the New Testament can be read from the standpoint of seeking models of discipleship that can be practised today. In contemporary Britain most people live in cities, a fact that raises the question how cities affected the life of Jesus and the first Christians. This question has provoked a surge of scholarship in the past 20 years or so, research that is fully represented in the second part of the book. A further point is that the author of the second part, John Vincent, is a leading figure in the movement to work out how New Testament discipleship can be practised in urban Britain today. This has found expression in the work of the Urban Theology Unit in Sheffield, which he founded, and of which he was the director for many years.

At the end of the book is an Epilogue entitled "Making Connections", which is based upon a method used at the Urban Theology Unit and derived from Liberation Theology. It involves analysing the situation of readers, followed by a movement from the situation to the biblical text and then a movement back to the situation. Some readers may well want to begin their reading by referring to this section; but I have put it at the end so that readers can decide for themselves how they wish to use the book.

I have been associated with the Urban Theology Unit in a small way for nearly 30 years and during that time have had regular contact with John Vincent. It has been a pleasure and a privilege to be able to co-operate with him in the writing of the present volume.

J. W. Rogerson
July 2008

Part 1

THE CITY IN THE OLD TESTAMENT

J. W. Rogerson

INTRODUCTION

The word "city" is not easy to define. There is no equivalent in French or German, where the words "ville" or "Stadt" can be translated as either city or town. A popular misconception in Britain is that a city is a place with a cathedral. This is disproved by the fact that Southwell and Southwark have cathedrals but are not cities, and that Cambridge and Cardiff are cities but do not have cathedrals. These examples could be multiplied. Strictly speaking, a city in Britain is a settlement that has been given a charter entitling it to call itself a city. This often has its roots in past history so that some cities are comparatively small and unimportant politically or economically (such as Durham), while others are the opposite (such as Birmingham, Manchester and Liverpool).

The same problem of definition is to be found in the Old Testament. Students who are beginning Hebrew are usually taught that *'īr* means city, ignoring the fact that "city" in English is difficult to define! In fact, the Hebrew word *'īr* can be used in many different ways. It can be used without qualification, for example, of Jericho in Joshua 6:3, where English translations render the word as "city". It can also be used, with an appropriate adjective, to describe unwalled villages, as in Deuteronomy 3:4 or fortified cities, as in 2 Kings 17:9.

The strict answer to the question "What is a city?" is that it is a word that can be used in a number of different ways to refer to human settlements that may vary considerably among themselves. However, this is not a complete, or even satisfactory, answer. The word "city" has acquired a good deal of emotional and other baggage. For some users of English, the word will suggest crime, traffic congestion, deprived areas and ethnic tensions. Others may think of theatres, prestigious shops and stores, specialist retail quarters and famous restaurants. While this may seem to open up a gap between the experience of life in biblical and in modern times, this may be more apparent than real. The question, why what the Bible contains about cities (however understood) should be of any interest to modern readers or citizens, is a very proper one. It can begin to be answered in the following way.

When modern users of English associate the word "city" with the factors mentioned above, they are pointing to the fact that cities (or large towns; but I shall continue to use the word "city") are places where power and resources are concentrated. The industrial revolution in Britain saw the creation of cities as centres of manufacturing and trade. Textiles, iron and steel, ship building, trading in things such as tea and sugar, led to the creation of modern industrial cities, leading to enormous increases in wealth and population as well as poverty and crime. Even though Britain is now a largely de-industrialized country, its former industrial cities remain centres of wealth, power and resources together with the many social and other problems that such concentration brings with it.

Again, at first sight this seems so different from the situation in biblical times that the question has to be asked how the Bible can have any bearing upon the city in the modern world. Most people in ancient Israel did not live in cities and, as will be described later, some of the Israelite cities, in any case, had little space for people actually to live in. But, like modern cities, Israelite cities were places where power and resources were concentrated. They were the centres where justice was administered, trade carried on, records kept, scribes trained, armies recruited, labour organized, power exercised. Although they did not touch the lives of ordinary people in the way that modern cities affect today's world (it is estimated that by 2025 60 per cent of the world's inhabitants will be urban dwellers; see Giddens, 1992: 292–301) they attracted the attention of Old Testament prophets and writers in a significant way. As centres of power and administration they determined the character of the nation they represented. The values and ideals of those in power in the cities often came in to conflict with prophetic and prophetically-inspired hopes for a nation supposedly loyal to a God of justice. The city, as referred to in the Old Testament, thus became a powerful and necessarily ambiguous symbol. As an institution that summed up human nature in all its selfishness and destructive inhumanity, it was described as having been founded by Cain, who murdered his brother Abel (Gen. 4:17). As an institution which, justly and rightly governed in obedience to God, could be a blessing to humanity, it became a symbol of hope for the nations of the world (Isa. 2:2–4/Mic. 4:1–4). In what follows, there will be two main sections. The first, based upon archaeology, will describe Israelite cities: their size, nature and functions. The second section will be based upon Old Testament texts that deal in different ways with the theme or ideas of the city. A closing section will draw conclusions.

Chapter 1

THE ISRAELITE CITY: HISTORY AND ARCHAEOLOGY

The Israelites did not invent cities and city life; they took over institutions that had existed for at least two thousand years before the heyday of Israelite cities (c. 925–720 BCE). The distinctively Israelite contribution was the prophetically-derived critique of cities and city life based upon belief in a God of justice. Urbanization in ancient Palestine began around 3000 BCE, with settlements such as Jericho and Megiddo which were characterized by large public buildings, including temples (see generally Fritz, 1990: 15–38). The urbanization process reached its peak around 2650–2350, and then underwent a decline, with many cities disappearing by around 2000. The causes are unknown. They could have included a decrease in rainfall, and a lowering of water tables, and inter-city rivalry and warfare. A second phase of urban expansion and subsequent decline took place in the period 1800–1200 BCE.

Israelite cities took over and rebuilt existing cities. This is true, apparently, even of Samaria, where the Bible gives the impression that it was a completely new foundation built on the initiative of the Israelite king Omri (see 1 Kgs 16:24; de Geus, 2003: 43). The striking thing about the Israelite cities is how much smaller they were than the most important centres of population in the ancient Near East. Also, some Israelite cities, such as Hazor, occupied only a small part of the site that had made up the preceding Canaanite city. Tables 1.1 and 1.2 give some idea of the size of Israelite cities compared with other settlements. Although the figures are estimates and in some cases (e.g. that of Jerusalem) controversial, they give a general indication of the state of affairs. The figures are hectares (a hectare being 2.47 acres).

The small size of Israelite cities raises the question of the number of their inhabitants. This is a matter fraught with complications. It has been argued that cities such as Megiddo, Samaria and Hazor during the period 925–720 had some 80 per cent of their space occupied by public buildings, the remaining space being open to accommodate fairs, pilgrims, armies

Table 1.1

Nineveh (seventh century)	2,041
Mari	283
Ugarit	36
Jerusalem (in the time of David)	6
Jerusalem (in the time of Hezekiah, late eighth century)	30
Hazor (Canaanite)	82
Hazor (Israelite)	12
Gibeon	11
Gezer	11
Lachish	7.5
Samaria	7.5
Megiddo	6
Shechem	4 or 5
Shiloh	3.5

and residents from surrounding areas in time of danger. At the same time, administrative centres such as Megiddo, Samaria and Hazor could hardly have functioned without an adequate number of personnel. These people probably lived outside the cities, either in the immediate vicinity in quarters whose remains have not been preserved, or in nearby villages whose buildings have suffered a similar fate (see de Geus, 2003: 179–80). Broshi and Gophna (1986) have suggested an average density of around 250 inhabitants per hectare in the pre-modern Near East. Bearing in mind the difficulties outlined above, this would give the following rough populations for Israelite cities:

These figures may have no value at all. On the other hand they may serve to alert us to the fact that when we think about Israelite cities we must think in terms of small units that do not resemble anything comparable to modern urban experience.

Table 1.2

Jerusalem (time of David)	1,500
Jerusalem (time of Hezekiah)	7,500
Hazor	3,000
Gibeon	2,750
Gezer	2,750
Lachish	1,875
Samaria	1,875
Megiddo	1,500
Shechem	1,000 to 1,250
Shiloh	875

De Geus has suggested that an Iron Age city in Palestine may have resembled a mediaeval European city in some respects. Similarities would include the city walls, with the highest part of the complex dominated by a castle and perhaps a cathedral in a mediaeval city, and by a fortress and palace or residence in the Iron Age case. The height of the wall and of the most important buildings would be intended to impress the local population and to deter potential enemies (de Geus, 2003: 167–68). Differences would include the fact that in Iron Age cities trade, justice and perhaps religious ceremonies (de Geus, 2003: 37–39) were carried on at the city gate and spaces immediately adjacent to it, while there would have been a special building for these activities in the mediaeval counterpart. The comparison between the Iron Age and mediaeval city enables the main functions and characteristics of the Israelite city to be listed (for what follows see de Geus, 2003: 171).

1. It housed or made possible the work of specialists, such as administrators, scribes or religious functionaries, all of whom were not primarily engaged in the production of food.
2. It contained public buildings used for collecting and distributing resources such as taxes.
3. It was a centre for trade and for the location of specialist services such as those provided by potters, smiths, metal workers and scribes.
4. It was a centre for the administration of justice.
5. Although probably governed by the heads of powerful families, it was a society constituted by allegiance to the city and its functions, rather than one based entirely upon kinship, and it exhibited distinctions based upon class (i.e. wealth).

The next chapter will deal with biblical texts that treat the theme of the city theologically. For the moment, some biblical passages will be examined which can be better understood in the light of modern knowledge of Iron Age cities.

The story of Noah in Genesis 6–9 is not obviously concerned with a city, and is not even located anywhere. It is also based upon, or shares traditions common with, other flood stories known from the ancient Near East (see Rogerson and Davies, 2005: 120–22). However, hearers or readers of the biblical story would arguably have connected it with a city because of the special skills implied in the construction of the ark. It is unlikely that one man would have combined the skills of carpenter, ship designer, and expert in the application of pitch, to mention only those detailed in the narrative. The acquisition of the wood and the pitch, necessary for the ark's construction, not to mention the purchase of the food for the ark's crew and animals, would have required the combination of trading and the transporting of materials that only a city could have organized. Of course, the story is not historical; but for hearers and readers it implied a level of human organization and co-operation that was arguably more apparent to people in the ancient world than to modern westerners, who take it for granted that the materials they may require for DIY work in the home will be readily available in a large warehouse-type store.

The story of Sodom in Genesis 19 describes Lot as sitting in the city's gate. Because Lot greets the two angelic visitors when they reach the city it might be concluded that he was sitting alone at the gate. This would be a mistake. The gate of a city was a complex of fortified buildings designed to give maximum protection in times of danger and easiest access on other occasions. A space, or square, either between two gate complexes or on the inside of them, was the principle area in a city where justice was administered (see Ruth 4:1–2) and trade carried on. It is most unlikely that Lot would be sitting alone in the square at the gate. Again, the story is not historical but the conventions shared by the author and hearers/readers would assume that Lot was sitting with other men, who would observe the arrival of the unusual visitors. The visitors initially decline Lot's invitation to his home and say that they will spend the night "in the street" (RSV). Later versions, such as the NRSV, have, rightly, "in the square". The visitors were not planning to sleep rough. It would not be unusual for visitors to spend the night in the square. The gates would be closed for protection against marauders and wild animals, and there were no inns or hostelries. Perhaps the story implies that it was the fact that Lot took the men into his house that aroused the curiosity of the inhabitants of the city. The narrative also plays upon the fact that Lot's position in the city is that of a sojourner (Gen. 19:9) rather than an established citizen. That, in these circumstances, he possessed a house in the city may have been a function of his wealth. Although the details discussed here are not central to the narrative, they are not without interest, and warn modern readers against reading their own city-dwelling experiences into the narrative.

In the Jubilee law of Leviticus 25:29–31 a distinction is made between a house in a walled city and one in a village with no wall. The former type of house, if sold, may be bought back by the vendor but only within one year of purchase. Thereafter it is the possession of the purchaser in perpetuity (unless, of course, the purchaser sells it after an interval of time) and it is not subject to the Jubilee law. The house in the unwalled village is subject to the Jubilee law, which means that it may be bought back at any time and, in any case, will revert to the original owner at the forty-ninth or fiftieth year. Part of the theological justification of the Jubilee is that the land belongs to God and that the use of it should reflect God's compassion. The economic forces that drive people into debt and slavery must not be allowed to establish permanent human conditions. Therefore, there should be periodic adjustments in order to restore dignity and independence to those who have fallen upon hard times. This is achieved, among other measures, by the restoration of lands to their original owners, lands that had been sold to meet debts.

Given this view, it is natural to ask why houses in walled cities should be treated differently from those in unwalled villages, and be exempted from the Jubilee laws. According to Noth (1965: 190) the distinction rested upon the persistence of 'ancient city law' that went back to 'Canaanite' times. Although Noth gives no evidence for this it has a certain plausibility. Given that Israelite cities were rarely, if ever, new foundations, certain rights and privileges may have been taken over from the pre-Israelite times. The question "who owns the city?" may have been impossible to answer; and it may have been that walled cities were believed to possess legal privileges (see de Geus, 2003: 23).

But there may also have been a simple, practical reason for the exemption. Israelite towns were very small in area, and although there may have been some free-standing houses of the four-roomed type, most houses were probably one-roomed dwellings with shared external walls. In some cases they were part of the casemate wall that surrounded the city. They were liable to damage and destruction from very heavy rains, not to mention siege and warfare (see generally de Geus, 2003: 17–18, 75–85). The right of re-purchase within a year made sense. If longer periods were specified, the house might no longer exist.

The story of the visit of the two Israelite spies to the house of Rahab the harlot in Jericho (Josh. 2:1–21) sheds interesting light on conditions in Israelite cities. Whatever view is taken of the historicity or otherwise of the story, it is meant to make sense to readers/hearers familiar with city life in the period of the monarchy. The two spies go to Jericho and lodge with Rahab. Israelite cities (in the narrative, of course, Jericho is a Canaanite city soon to be destroyed; but the narrative assumes that Jericho is like an Israelite city) were very small and probably did not have inns or guest-houses. A harlot, however, had rooms in which to pursue her profession, one which was accepted without comment or condemnation. If two spies wanted to cover their tracks and intentions, a visit to a harlot's house would give them that necessary cover. However, the spies would have to pass through the city gate, and could not do this unnoticed. Their presence at Rahab's house is reported to the king, who demands their exposure. Rahab lies by admitting that she was visited but claims that her clients left just before the city gate closed. She has, in fact, hidden the men on the roof of her house.

The mention of the roof raises the question of the nature and height of Israelite houses. De Geus argues that it is becoming increasingly accepted that Israelite houses had two storeys possibly topped by an upper room as a third storey. The roof would probably be atop the second storey, with a parapet providing safety for users (cp. Deut. 22:8 and 2 Kgs 1:2–4 where king Ahaziah is seriously injured by falling from his upper chamber). In the Rahab story the spies are hidden by her among bundles of flax that are presumably on the roof in order to dry out before being made into linen. As soon as it is safe to do so, the spies are let down by a rope through a window. This assumes that Rahab's house is built into the casemate wall surrounding the city. The window is an opening that would be closed, most likely by a wooden lattice. Upon this lattice she binds a scarlet cord so that she can be identified and spared when the Israelites capture the city (cp. Josh. 6:17, 22–25). Rahab's family is also spared. She would not have lived alone in what the narrative implies must have been a house with a number of rooms, even if there was also space for her to provide a service to her clients.

Judges 19 shares many similarities with Genesis 19, of which the following are relevant to the present discussion. A Levite is travelling with his concubine (a wife who is either of slave status or, if not a slave, not the man's primary wife) from Bethlehem to the hill country of Ephraim. As night draws on they make for Gibeah, and prepare to spend the night in the square at the gate of the city because no one offers them hospitality. Although this may sound dangerous from a modern city perspective, it has already been pointed out above that in an Israelite city the square was a small public space protected by the closure of the city gate in the evening, with further security ensured by the presence at the gate of watchmen charged with the safety of the city during the hours of darkness. However, an old man who comes from the hill country of Ephraim (and who thus has at least a geographical or even kin connection with the Levite) and who is temporarily residing in Gibeah, offers them hospitality. This becomes the occasion for the outrage at Gibeah, in which the Levite's concubine is given to the "base fellows" of the city to be raped all through the night. Attention is drawn to the fact that the man who offered the hospitality was a sojourner, that is, someone voluntarily or forcefully separated from his own kinship group. The fact that he is described as old (Judg. 19:16) yet as possessing a field in the neighbourhood and a house in the city suggests that he was a long-term inhabitant of the city. Those who dwelt in it did not have common kinship; yet the fact that he was an "outsider" may have been the reason why his guests were abused and why he apparently had no one to defend him in the city against its "base fellows".

An earlier incident in Judges 3:19–23 gives information about the accommodation occupied by a "king", presumably in the "city of palms" (Judg. 3:13), i.e. Jericho. Ehud, of the tribe of Benjamin, is deputed to take tribute to Eglon, to Jericho, and in the course of the transactions he gains a private audience with Eglon "in his cool roof chamber" (Judg. 3: 20). This was presumably a special room on the roof of a two-storey building, with windows on all four walls to allow the wind to blow through. It also had a closet containing a toilet (Judg. 3:24) from which the excrement went through a passage in the outside wall to a pit. The remains of a toilet emptying into a cesspit have apparently been found in the so-called house of Ahiel in Jerusalem (King and Stager, 2001: 70–71). Ehud takes advantage of his private interview to kill Eglon, and leaves the chamber, locking the doors behind him. The lock consisted of a wooden bolt that could be locked into place by pins that fell into a gap in the bolt from a kind of box above the bolt. The key was inserted into a slot in the bolt and pushed the pins in the bolt upwards, so that the bolt could be freely moved (see King and Stager, 2001: 33 for an illustration). A hole in the door enabled a person to insert a hand from the outside through the door so as to grasp the bolt or apply the key. The narrative implies that the bolt and lock were on the outside of the doors in relation to the chamber, which is why Ehud could lock the doors as he left simply by pushing the bolt. The narrative also implies that Eglon locked the doors whenever he used the closet, which he could do from the inside by passing this hand through the hole in the door. The servants, seeing the locked doors assumed that Eglon had done this to ensure privacy. Only after too much time had passed did they become anxious, produce the key to unlock the door, and discover their dead master.

The story of the siege of Samaria in 2 Kgs 6:24–7:20 gives a vivid picture of what could happen to a city in time of war. Although it is not impossible that the events described actually took place in Samaria, the conditions depicted could have occurred in any important city, and hearers/readers of the story would have related it to their own knowledge and experience of cites whether they had been to Samaria or not. There is no need to seek to correlate the story with what is (incompletely) known about Samaria from excavations.

Although cities possessed storage facilities and secure access to water, it did not mean that they could sustain for very long a swollen population driven to take shelter in the city in the face of an attack by a large army. This is what the account in 2 Kings 6:24–7:20 presupposes. There was not a general famine in the land, because the besieging army, which lived off the land, was well supplied with food, as the four "lepers" discovered when they decided to visit the Syrian camp and found it abandoned. Also, the fact that, as soon as it was discovered that the siege had been lifted, prices returned to normal, shows that the famine was caused simply by the fact that the people in the city had access to only what could be found there (cp. 2 Kgs 7:8; 16). The siege would have emphasized the difference between rich and poor. The king's household would survive, if necessary, by eating the horses kept in the city, of which five remained when the siege was lifted (2 Kgs 7:13). The fact that an ass's head could be bought for 80 silver shekels and a quarter of a kab of dove's dung (possibly fuel, or a substitute for salt or the corruption of a word for "carob pods"; see Gray, 1964: 471) for five silver shekels indicates that those wealthy enough to do so could purchase admittedly not ideal means of sustenance. Also, some traders used the circumstances not to practise solidarity with the hungering population, but to exploit them massively. The poor had to resort to desperate measures, as in the case of the two women reduced to eating the flesh of their own child (2 Kgs 6:28–29).

It was to the king as he passed by upon the city wall that one of the unfortunate women cried out for help (2 Kgs 6:26). De Geus (2003: 17–18) notes that casemate city walls were sufficiently wide for defenders to use them to move from one part of the city to another as attacks developed. Even an Israelite city *not* packed with people seeking protection would not provide easy and quick access from one section to another. The wall was an essential means of movement around the city when it was besieged. Also, the wall might be widened in the time of siege by wooden platforms that enabled defenders to drop stones or boiling oil on attackers beneath.

In its present form, the narrative is centred upon the extraordinary deeds of Elisha, whom the king holds responsible for the parlous state of affairs, presumably on the ground that Elisha is responsible for the failure of God to take action on behalf of the city (cp. 2 Kgs 6:31). The centrepiece of the narrative is Elisha's prophecy that the siege will be lifted the next day, but that the king's captain, who doubts Elisha's word, will see this without benefiting from it. This word is fulfilled when the captain is killed as the people rush and struggle to get through the gate when they learn that the Syrian army has gone away. City gates were narrow, and sometimes placed parallel to the city walls so that an invading army could be attacked from the walls if it penetrated the gate. A sharp turn then brought the gateway into the city. Any modern reader who has been part of a large crowd trying to negotiate a narrow space will readily appreciate that there could be at least one fatality, if not more, as people rushed from the city, to try to get to where food was available. The end of the siege meant a return to normal trading in the gate, i.e. the square in the vicinity of the gate or gates (2 Kgs 7:16).

Accounts of three more sieges occur in 2 Kings 17 to 25. The first is a brief notice to the effect that the Assyrians laid siege to Samaria for three years before it was finally captured (2 Kgs 17:5–6). Presumably the final days of the siege witnessed shortages as desperate as those described in the Elisha incident just discussed. However, the three-year siege, as well as the eight-month siege of Jerusalem in 587 (2 Kgs 25:1–3) shows that a well-prepared city could hold out for some considerable time. Among the tactics that could be used to undermine a city's resistance was propaganda, as 2 Kings 18:19–25, 28–35 shows. During the siege of Jerusalem by the Assyrians in 701 BCE an Assyrian spokesman comes close enough to the city wall to address the defenders. Wherever the upper pool and Fuller's Field may have been (see 2 Kgs 18:17) the narrative demands that they are within hearing distance of the wall. The Assyrian propagandist uses several arguments, including the claim that the God of Israel has told the Assyrian king to capture the city (2 Kgs 18:25). He also lists the cities that had succumbed to the Assyrians, to support his case for the futility of further resistance (2 Kgs 18:34). Although the narrative can hardly contain the words actually spoken by an Assyrian propagandist, they are plausible from the point of view of the narrative.

The account of the siege of Jerusalem in 587 BCE (2 Kgs 25:1–12) notes that the food in the city had run out and that the city wall had been breached. De Geus (2003: 20) points out that Assyrian battering rams were huge crowbars designed to lever stones out of the wall, and the same can be presumed for the Babylonians. He also notes (2003: 33) that cities had small postern gates that could be concealed in time of war. It was presumably through one of these that king Zedekiah tried unsuccessfully to escape by night after the Babylonians had breached the city (2 Kgs 25:4).

The accounts of sieges do not mention a shortage of water. This was because, in a land where no rain fell between April/May and September/October (in good years!), it was impossible for any city to be established on a site which did not either have secure access to a spring or secure access to the water table. Extensive water systems giving access to the water table from within the city walls have been discovered at Hazor and Megiddo, dating probably from the ninth century. Jerusalem was supplied by a spring named Gihon, or "gusher". Access to this was by way of a shaft within the city. Also, a tunnel some 550 metres long conducted the waters to the foot of the hill to the west of the city.

The shaft and tunnel in Jerusalem have provoked much discussion. Some experts have seen a reference to the shaft at 2 Samuel 5:8, a view reflected in translations such as the RSV, NRSV, NIV and REB which present David as encouraging his soldiers to attack the city by climbing up the shaft. Some of the difficulties of this view are set out by de Geus (2003: 128) and can be summarized as follows. Experiments in which experienced climbers tried to climb up the shaft have indicated that while the task is not impossible, it is unlikely to have been undertaken. The date of the shaft is uncertain. If it did exist during the presumed time of David, entry to it from outside the city would be unlikely. The defenders would have blocked and concealed any entrance. There is the additional problem of the meaning of the word translated "water shaft" and the Hebrew verb which precedes it. The verb translated as "get up" (e.g. by NRSV) usually means "to smite" and because the noun (translated by NRSV as "water shaft") can mean a hook, some have taken it to refer to some kind of weapon. The NEB translates it as "grappling iron".

The tunnel has similarly caused controversy. Second Kings 20:20 credits king Hezekiah with making the pool and conduit, and thus bringing water into the city. The "conduit" could be a reference to the tunnel, but if the shaft already existed it is not easy to see why the tunnel was needed, unless its purpose was to bring water to the western hill, which was now beginning to be built upon. Second Chronicles 32:30 says that Hezekiah "closed the upper outlet of the waters of Gihon and directed them down to the west side of the city of David". This notice may reflect conditions at the time of composition of Chronicles (late fourth century BCE), with Hezekiah being credited, on the basis of 2 Kings 20:20, with work that was possibly carried out much later than his time. An inscription discovered at the western end of the tunnel in the 1880s, referring to the construction of the tunnel, makes no mention of Hezekiah, nor indeed of any other circumstance connected with its construction, and was surmounted by words in Greek, which seem to have been obliterated when the inscription was cut out of the rock to be taken to the museum in Istanbul.

The previous pages, which have dealt with sieges, may seem to have little bearing upon today's world. However, within living memory, wars have included sieges, which have brought great suffering upon those involved. The siege of Stalingrad, which lasted from early September 1942 to late January 1943 is the best known, being followed by another kind of siege, the encirclement of the German Sixth Army that had been attacking Stalingrad. But the war also produced other types of siege, especially in the form of the ghettos such as that in Warsaw, into which Jews were herded and secluded. The present situation in Iraq has produced yet another type of siege: the heavily-guarded security areas occupied by top government and army officials and diplomats. What all this shows is that because cities are centres of power and resources they become prime targets in any human conflict. To control them is to control the people who depend upon then. To eliminate them, as can be done in modern warfare from the safety of the air or from sea-based launching pads, is likewise to destroy the power that they both symbolize and actualize. Cities are in fact conquered or destroyed by other cities, even in today's world. They can and do become centres for the accumulation of destructive power and of the will to unleash that power on others.

A narrative that illustrates the connection between cities and power is the account of the re-building of Jerusalem by Nehemiah in Nehemiah 2:11–4:23; 11:1–2. These chapters are generally held to come from the Nehemiah Memorial, an apparently autobiographical source, written after 432 BCE and incorporated into the book of Nehemiah, with some editing, around 400–350 BCE. If the dates in the book can be relied upon, Nehemiah came to Jerusalem from Susa around 445, saw the ruined state of Jerusalem, and organized the population to restore it. Whether attempts had been made to rebuild the city or parts of it following its destruction by the Babylonians in 587 is not known. Ezra 3 records the rebuilding of the temple, an event usually dated to 515 BCE, while Haggai, in an oracle usually dated to 522 criticizes the people for rebuilding their own houses while at the same time the temple remains in ruins. It is difficult to suppose that for around 140 years (from 587 to 445) nobody did anything with or about the ruins of Jerusalem. According to Nehemiah 2:14, Nehemiah was unable to ride along the Kidron Valley on the eastern side of Jerusalem because of the debris that lay there. A possible solution is that what Nehemiah saw was the result of recent action against Jerusalem taken by the authorities in Samaria, who were opposed to an attempt to restore to Jerusalem any position of authority in the region.

Whatever may have been the background to Nehemiah's work, several things are noteworthy. First, the work of repairing or rebuilding walls was partly undertaken by families living in the city close to the wall. Thus Nehemiah 3:10 states that "Jedaiah the son of Harumaph repaired opposite his house; and next to him Hattush the son of Hashabneiah repaired". This would make sense if the repairs that they undertook were to recently-inflicted damage. It is difficult to accept that families would want to live in houses with no city wall to protect them from wild animals or thieves. There is also a mention of specialized trades. Goldsmiths and perfumers are mentioned at Nehemiah 3:8, purveyors of trades that suggest that Jerusalem had not been permanently in ruins for 140 years previously.

It is striking that so many gates are mentioned in the narrative – ten in all. This would appear to be an excessively large number, and may suggest that the rebuilding after 587 had not been allowed to become fortified by walls that had only one main defensive gate. However, the rebuilding in Nehemiah 3 emphasizes the protective function of the gates, however or whatever they may have been prior to this time. Thus "the sons of Hassenaah built the Fish Gate; they laid its beams and set its doors, its bolts and its bars" (Neh. 3:3; and cp. vv 6.12. 14.15). After the completion of the city, steps were taken to increase Jerusalem's population by moving a tenth of the people living in surrounding towns and villages into the city (Neh. 11:1–2). This increased the population to something under 5,000 according to Otto (1980: 108) or perhaps 3,000 according to Grabbe (2004: 302). Grabbe, indeed, makes some pertinent observations about the rebuilding of the city walls in relation to Nehemiah's mission:

> A city wall can have an important social function. It can serve to enclose people into communities and bond them together; it can be used to hold the outside world at arm's length. A wall can also be a means of controlling those enclosed by it; it can close people off into a ghetto. (Grabbe, 2004: 307–08)

Grabbe goes on to point out that the rebuilding of the city enabled Nehemiah to control those who worked and lived in it and, by implication, the Jewish province over which it now claimed authority. '[T]he city wall – as mundane as it might seem – was far more than just an architectural project; it was essential to Nehemiah's reforms' (Grabbe, 2004: 308).

But if cities in the biblical (and no doubt, ancient) world were instruments of power, they could also be places where criticism of that power could be developed and articulated. Bourdieu (1977: 233 note 16) points out that in cities the coming together of people with differing outlooks or even different cultural traditions, can lead to the questioning of what is taken for granted, or of prevailing opinions. Old Testament narratives can certainly be appreciated in this light.

The Elijah cycle of stories mentions a certain Obadiah who was "over the household" and who actually opposed the policies of Ahab and his foreign Queen Jezebel by secretly hiding and feeding prophets who were loyal to the God of Israel (see 1 Kgs 18: 3–4). Obadiah's position as royal chamberlain put him in possession of resources which he was able to use to counteract the policies of Jezebel. We should not suppose that he acted alone. He would have been supported by administrators and servants who either agreed with his policy or were sufficiently loyal to or frightened of Obadiah to be willing to do things that would probably have been punishable by death if they had become known.

Something of the same tension is explicit in the narrative of the time of the fall of Jerusalem in 597–587 BCE. Passages in 2 Kings 22; 25:22–26 and Jeremiah 36–41 indicate that two powerful families with differing viewpoints played an important role in shaping the policies of the kings and nobles during this crucial period (see further Rogerson and Davies, 2005: 28–29). The two families are those of Elishama, the state secretary in around 605 BCE, when Jeremiah dictated his prophecies to Baruch (Jer. 36:20) and Shaphan, who was secretary in 622 when the book of the law was discovered in the temple in the reign of Josiah (2 Kgs 22:3–10). A son of Shaphan, Elasa, takes Jeremiah's letter to the exiles in Babylon (Jer. 29:3) while another son, Ahikam, protects Jeremiah when his prophecies about the impending fate of Jerusalem put his life in danger (Jer. 26:24). Ahikam's son, Gedaliah, is appointed to be governor of the area by the Babylonians following their conquest of Jerusalem (Jer. 39:13–14; 2 Kgs 25:22). However, Gedaliah is assassinated by the grandson of Elishama, erstwhile head of the family that opposed the family of Shaphan (Jer. 41:1–3; 2 Kgs 25:25). These traditions indicate a pro-Jeremiah faction that favoured an accommodation with Babylon in the belief that God was using Babylon to punish Judah (cp. Jer. 38:17–28) and a faction that regarded such sentiments as disloyalty to the nation. Such differences of opinion, and the actions to which they led, could only have been possible in the context of a city, and the power that cities enabled certain factions to acquire.

Another example of the social critiques that the city made possible is provided by the book of Ecclesiastes (or Qoheleth, to give it its Hebrew name). Indeed, the implied author, writing around 300 BCE under the assumed identity of a former king in Jerusalem, emphasizes the privileges he enjoyed in Jerusalem, so as to be able to draw attention to the darker sides of life in a city:

> I made great works; I built houses and planted vineyards for myself; I made myself gardens and parks, and planted in them all kinds of fruit trees. I made myself pools from which to water the forest of growing trees. I bought male and female slaves … I had also great possessions of herds and flocks, more than any who had been before me in Jerusalem. I also gathered for myself silver and gold and the treasure of kings and provinces … Then I considered

all that my hands had done and the toil I had spent in doing it, and behold, all
was vanity and a striving after wind. (Eccl. 2:4–8a, 11)

The writer's disillusionment is not simply a feeling of personal emptiness,
unfulfilled by the material advantages he had enjoyed. He also has an acute
awareness of the unfairnesses of life, and of the apparent human inability
to do anything about them. When he writes:

I saw under the sun that in the place of justice even there was wickedness,
and in the place of righteousness, even there was wickedness (Eccl. 3:16)

it must not be forgotten that according to the implied circumstances of
the book, the writer was a powerful king, who was therefore directly or
indirectly responsible for the state of affairs that he so movingly described.
The same is true of the complaint:

Again I saw all the oppressions that are practised under the sun. And behold
the tears of the oppressed, and they had no one to comfort them! On the side
of their oppressors there was power, and there was no one to comfort them.
(Eccl. 4:1)

What this amounts to, then, is a searching commentary on the failure of
humanity to be truly human. The city enables the writer to observe these
facts, but it also affords him the opportunity to criticize them. He is also
able to add a touching illustration of the permanent value of wisdom,
based upon a story concerning a siege.

There was a little city with few men in it; and a great king came against it and
besieged it, building great siegeworks against it. But there was found in it a
poor wise man, and he by his wisdom delivered the city. Yet no one remembered
that poor man. But I say that wisdom is better than might, though the poor
man's wisdom is despised, and his words are not heeded. (Eccl. 9:14–16)

A cameo of the various trades that were essential to city life is found in
Ecclesiasticus (Sirach) 38: 24–34. The writer is, in fact, somewhat
contemptuous of those whose work he describes, because he considers a
scribe to stand at the summit of human endeavours. Nonetheless he admits
that "without them a city cannot be established, and men can neither
sojourn nor live there" (Ecclesiasticus 38: 32). Who are the "them"? They
are the craftsmen "who cut the signets of seals" the smith who forges iron
and the potter who moulds the clay. That these craftsmen are skilful and
diligent is readily admitted by the writer. Yet such people:

are not sought out for the council of the people,
nor do they attain eminence in the public assembly.
They do not sit in the judge's seat,

nor do they understand the sentence of judgement;
they cannot expound discipline or judgement,
and they are not found using proverbs.
(Ecclesiasticus 38: 32–6)

These words are an indication that cities were active producers of class distinctions. Those who practised crafts upon which the predominantly agricultural population depended – especially smiths and potters – had something to exchange for the food produced by others. This was not so obviously the case with administrators, scribes and judges (if the latter were specialists in matters of law). The writer of Ecclesiasticus cannot be commended for his patronizing attitude towards those whose practical skills were so important in maintaining the fabric of life in the city. We can be grateful to him, however, for his honesty in indicating an aspect of city life which human nature could take advantage of in an anti-humanitarian way.

The same is true of the passage in Proverbs 7, with its vivid description of the "loose woman" and its warning to young men not to be led astray by her. Modern readers will want to note that there would not be "loose women" unless they were encouraged by men to be so. The writer looks from his lattice window:

at the shadow of my house
I have looked out through my lattice,
and I have perceived among the youths,
a young man without sense,
passing along the street near her corner,
taking the road to her house
in the twilight, in the evening,
at the time of night and darkness.
(Prov. 7:6–9)

The "loose woman" meets him and entices him with such sentiments as "my husband is not at home" and that she had specially covered her couch with rich furnishings and perfumed spices so that they might make love throughout the night. His falling to these temptations is described as "an ox [that] goes to the slaughter" or "a stag … caught fast" and as a bird that rushes into a snare (Prov. 7:22–3). It should be noted that attempts have been made to describe the "loose woman" as a devotee of Aphrodite, or as a foreign woman, so that what is being warned against is either idolatry or consorting with "outsiders", or both (for a full discussion see McKane, 1970: 334–41). While a "straightforward" reading of the text is not free from difficulties (there are some interesting variants in the ancient Greek version known as the Septuagint) it is less problematic than the reconstruction in terms of cult prostitution or the fatal attractions of exotic foreign women. For present purposes, however the text is understood, it provides evidence for the city as an ambiguous moral sphere in which human weaknesses could be exploited and relationships destroyed.

Chapter 2

THE ISRAELITE CITY – BIBLICAL PERSPECTIVES

1. The Founding of the First City, Genesis 4:1–24.

The biblical writers were almost certainly aware of the fact that the city was not an Israelite invention. Israelites who travelled, whether as soldiers or exiles, saw that other nations had cities; cities that in some cases (e.g. Babylon) were far bigger and more magnificent than anything to be found in ancient Israel. The story of the founding of the first city in Genesis 4 has therefore to do with the city as a universal phenomenon. Yet while the opening chapters of Genesis describe the origins of a world and human culture of which the Israelites were only a small part, that description was framed in terms of the distinctive theological understanding of reality that the biblical writers embraced. Cain and Abel were not Israelites, and their quarrel, and the murder of Abel by his brother Cain have been compared with the story of Romulus and Remus (see Westermann, 1970: 390), and the founding of Rome. While the biblical story may well owe something to common folk tales about conflicts between brothers, in its present form it expresses Israelite religious convictions about the nature of cities. From this perspective, the city as a human institution is characterized not by brotherly co-operation, but by a rivalry that leads to bloodshed.

Studies of the narrative of Genesis 4:1–24 have emphasized the importance in it of the word "brother" (Rogerson 1991: 33). It occurs six times in verses 8 to 11, in the passage that relates Cain's murder of Abel and his attempts to cover up and deny responsibility for what he has done. The point is emphasized that Cain has acted in a manner that has betrayed the bond that ought to exist between him and his brother. Further, he is without hope in the world, and his future existence is made possible only by the fact that against all odds, God is prepared to offer him protection (Gen. 4:15).

The account of the building of the first city immediately follows. Experts have argued about the transmission of the text of Genesis 4:17, and whether it originally implied that it was Enoch and not Cain who built the city (see

Westermann, 1970: 443–44). In its present form the text can only make Cain the founder. The fact that Cain is a murderer who owes his continuing life only to the mercy of God, imports an ambiguity into the nature of the first city. It exists by divine permission, permission granted to a person who had betrayed his brother and thus humanity. This is an ambiguity that runs like a constant thread through the biblical narratives that deal with cites.

Towards the end of Genesis 4 there occurs a poetic fragment spoken by Lamech. Lamech is a fifth-generation descendant of Cain and the husband of the two wives, Adah and Zillah, whose children become the ancestors of cattle breeders, musicians and metal workers. The point of this information is to indicate how human culture is developing. However, it is not the only thing that is developing. The poem reads:

> Adah and Zillah, hear my voice;
> you wives of Lamech, harken to what I say:
> I have slain a man for wounding me,
> A young man for striking me.
> If Cain is avenged sevenfold,
> truly Lamech seventy-sevenfold.

In spite of the mercy that God showed to Cain, this has not removed the violence endemic in the human race. Indeed, Lamech's boast to have exacted a "seventy-sevenfold" vengeance has made a mockery of the divine mercy shown to Cain. The advance of civilization and human culture has not been an unmixed blessing. It has given the human race, as represented by Lamech, an independent boldness to disregard human solidarity and to champion the rule of naked force. Given that the city in ancient Israel was the place which enabled civilization to advance, this founding story in Genesis exposes the dark side of the city, the city as the place where inhumanity can use the resources of the city for evil, not for good.

2. The City as the Symbol of Human Rebellion against God – Genesis 11:1–10.

The story usually known as the Tower of Babel is another narrative concerning the origin of the city. It is also more than that, because the narrative as we have it has combined several different motifs: (a) the building of a city and tower in order to establish something permanent on the earth (verses 2–4a); (b) the origin of different nations as the result of the builders being "scattered abroad upon the face of the ... earth" (verses 4b, 8); (c) the origin of different languages (verses 7–8); (d) the origin and meaning of the name Babel (verse 9). Although the motifs do not fit perfectly together, they are not entirely at odds. The desire to build a city so that the builders will not be scatted abroad fits with the desire "to make a name for ourselves" (verse 4b). Small villages or the tented encampments of herdsmen left no permanent evidence of the existence of their forebears to later generations. A city not only established bonds of obligation among its residents; it enabled wealth and culture to be passed from generation to generation.

Genesis 11 begins with people who apparently have no settled home until they find the plain in the land of Shinar and settle there. Shinar has already been mentioned in Genesis 10:10, where it is said to contain the towns of Babel, Erech and Accad. The readers/hearers of the story would presumably have identified Shinar with what we call Mesopotamia. The settlers decide to build a city. They have invented or discovered the making of bricks by baking clay, and by utilizing bitumen (which is found naturally in Mesopotamia) to bond the bricks together. The simple statement "come, let us build ourselves a city" (verse 4) should not make us suppose that there existed an ancient type of Building Co-operative, in which all the citizens rolled up their sleeves and helped with the work. Cities were built by forced labour (cp. Exod. 1:11), by one class of humans oppressing another. Slaves would be forced to collect the clay and straw for the bricks, and would also have the unenviable task of digging up or creaming off the layers of bitumen. The builders who wished to make a name for themselves did so at the expense of those who were forced to undertake the hardest work, who most likely did not enjoy liberty, and who were least likely to be able to make a name for themselves. The mention of the tower together with the city (verse 4) has led to the suggestion that a "city" tradition has been united with an independent "tower" tradition, but this is not likely. A fortified city would possess a tower-like fortress, and a tower that stood alone without being part of a city would make no sense. The function of the mention of the tower is to make possible the idea that the city will reach up to heaven, and thereby allow its inhabitants to invade the sphere of God.

In verses 5 and 6, God comes down to see the city and tower. He sees the unity and strength of the human race, takes fright as it were, and decides to scatter the human race and "confuse their language", that is, cause them to speak mutually unintelligible languages. These are the most difficult verses in the passage because they combine the originally distinct motifs of the origin of different languages, the existence of different peoples in different parts of the world (the "scattering abroad") and the existence of an unfinished city or tower (see verse 8 where it is said that the building was discontinued). This latter point, the unfinished building, has led commentators to speculate on whether part of the story originated to explain the existence of an unfinished building such as the Etemenanki Temple in Babylon which was begun by Nebuchadnezzar I (1123–1101), apparently never completed, and destroyed by Xerxes king of Persia following a rebellion of Babylon in 484–482 (see Rogerson and Davies, 2005: 122). With regard to the other motifs, the biblical writer was explaining the existence of difference languages and peoples by means of a story set in "beginning time", the time different from that of the writer and readers/hearers but in continuity with their time. By combining the motifs together, the writer was making the theological point that the unity of the human race was a threat to the divine order. This may sound odd to modern readers; but it must be remembered that the unity of the human race meant the unity of purpose of those who controlled human destiny. The achievement of their purpose involved the enslavement of other humans. It meant the disregarding of any belief in divine sanctions that might put a brake upon the exploitation and inhuman treatment of others. The divine fear evoked by the inspection of the building of the city was not simply that God would be displaced by human kind, but rather a fear of what that would mean for the world and the human race as a whole. This is a point that can easily be appreciated today in a world that has seen the rise of totalitarian dictators who have not scrupled to sacrifice millions of humans in order to achieve and sustain their malevolent ideologies and, in the case of dictators such as Hitler and Stalin, to realize their grandiose architectural ambitions. Genesis 11:1–9 gives a very negative view of the city as a place of human exploitation, and human aggrandisement at the expense of other humans.

3. Sodom – the City of Wrong

Apart from Jerusalem, no city is mentioned as frequently in the Old Testament as Sodom. Before the subject is pursued further, however, it is necessary to comment on the name Gomorrah, which is coupled with that of Sodom on 15 occasions, with the result that readers become familiar with the phrase "Sodom and Gomorrah". In fact, there are no passages that deal specifically with Gomorrah. In Genesis 13:12 Lot moves as far as Sodom and it is to Sodom that the angelic visitors come (Gen. 19:1). In the previous chapter Abraham argues with God about whether it would be right for Sodom to be destroyed if ten righteous people were to be found there

(Gen. 18:22–33). Nevertheless, when the destruction does take place, Gomorrah and other "cities of the valley" (Gen. 19:29) are also destroyed. The best way to deal with this apparent inconsistency is to say that the phrase "Sodom and Gomorrah" had become a standard formula in the language of the common people. The phrase probably had its origin in a natural disaster that destroyed the two cities. Where and when that was, is impossible to say with certainly. The two cities, together with the other "cities of the valley" have been variously located at the northern and southern ends of the Dead Sea, and one theory has identified Sodom with Bad edh-Dhra at the south-eastern edge of the Dead Sea.

What matters for present purposes is that Old Testament tradition took and built upon the name Sodom, without being able or necessarily wanting to dissociate it from the popular phrase "Sodom and Gomorrah". The accounts of wickedness dealt with Sodom only; the important symbolic use of the name usually included that of Gomorrah.

What was the wickedness of Sodom? The popular answer would be that it was male homosexuality – sodomy – to use the word in English that perpetuates the name of the city. A careful reading of the biblical text leads to other conclusions. In Genesis 19, the passage most readily connected with Sodom in popular thought, the wickedness is that of a potential public sexual orgy which does not, in fact, take place. The men of the city demand to have sexual access to the two visitors who have come to lodge with Lot. However, the visitors, who are angels, smite the would-be evildoers with blindness, thus frustrating their intention (Gen. 19:11). An explicit counter view is found in Ezekiel 16:46–49. In this remarkable passage, Sodom is described as the younger sister of Jerusalem, living to her south. Jerusalem is accused of not only reproducing Sodom's abominations, but of surpassing them. What were these abominations? According to Ezekiel 16:49:

> this was the guilt of your sister Sodom: she and her daughters had pride, surfeit of food, and prosperous ease, but did not aid the poor and needy.

The origin of this verdict is unknown. It may be an independent tradition or perhaps based upon the tradition in Genesis 13:10 that the part of the Jordan valley where Sodom was located was well watered. Nonetheless it needs to be set alongside Genesis 19 if justice is to be done to the content of the Bible.

Another passage that speaks of the wickedness of Sodom (and Gomorrah) is Jeremiah 23:14.

> But in the prophets of Jerusalem
> I have seen a horrible thing:
> they commit adultery and walk in lies;
> they strengthen the hands of evil-doers,
> so that no one turns from his wickedness;
> all of them have become like Sodom to me,
> and its inhabitants like Gomorrah.

The accusation against the prophets is that of heterosexual immorality, and deceit (they walk in lies). This deceit may be the preaching of peace when there is no peace (Jer. 6:14). The strengthening of the hands of evil-doers may be the failure to condemn social injustices. In becoming like Sodom and Gomorrah the prophets have committed a wide range of abuses, probably including social injustices. The passage incidentally provides one reason for the double appellation "Sodom and Gomorrah" – it enables the verse to be expressed in the parallelism of Hebrew poetry:

> all of them have become like Sodom to me,
> and its inhabitants like Gomorrah.

Summing up so far it can be said that the destruction of Sodom and Gomorrah had made these cities into a byword in popular thought and language, in the same way that the names Hiroshima and Auschwitz have become bywords in modern times for human destructiveness. In Hebrew tradition the destruction (whatever it was) that had wiped out the cities had been attributed to divine intervention, as a judgement upon human wickedness. What that wickedness had been was variously identified in the tradition, as has been explained.

The remarkable thing about Sodom and Gomorrah was the way in which the cities, epitomizing the greatest human wickedness, were used in the Old Testament to accuse other cities, particularly Jerusalem, of like wickedness. It has already been pointed out how in Ezekiel 16 Sodom is described as the younger sister of Jerusalem. In Isaiah 1:10 the rulers and citizens of Jerusalem are addressed as though they were the rulers and citizens of Sodom and Gomorrah in another passage which incidentally takes advantage of the two names in order to use the parallelism of Hebrew poetry:

> Hear the word of the LORD,
> you rulers of Sodom!
> Give ear to the teaching of our God,
> you people of Gomorrah!

The passage goes on to condemn the hollowness of the religious practices of the people and to command social justice:

> learn to do good;
> seek justice,
> correct oppression;
> defend the fatherless,
> plead for the widow. (Isa. 1:17)

Another application of the names Sodom and Gomorrah is to link them with their destruction, and then to say that other cities or countries will share the same fate. Thus Babylon is threatened with the fate of Sodom and Gomorrah in Isaiah 13:19 and Jeremiah 50:40, while Edom is the place targeted in Jeremiah 49:18. Zephaniah 2:9 (again using Hebrew poetic parallelism) says that Moab will become like Sodom and the Ammonites like Gomorrah. In Lamentations 4:6 the writer says that the chastisement of Jerusalem has been greater than the punishment of Sodom.

It is no accident that a city has been chosen to epitomize the sum of human wickedness. This could be said to be a trivial observation because if human wickedness is going to be found anywhere, this is most likely to be in the place where the concentration of human power makes greatest the opportunity for the abuse of fellow humans. Yet people in the ancient world had a great regard for cities, in the same way that people do in today's world; and no doubt ancient (as well as modern) visitors to cities hoped that they would not encounter the wicked aspects of the cities. Perhaps they were blind to the existence of this side of city life. In this respect, the Ezekiel 16 passage which describes the sin of Sodom as greed and unwillingness to assist the poor and needy becomes particularly significant. Red light and no-go areas in cities become infamous and can be avoided. A structural affluence built on the poverty of others is less easy to discern, and may even construct buildings and institutions that many will admire. The Old Testament traditions about Sodom invite readers to think profoundly rather than superficially about cities, and what it is that makes them bad and good.

4. The City and the Country – the Song of Songs

From the economic point of view the city and the country were mutually dependent. Cities did not produce food, while the specialist tradesmen who provided tools, pots, copper utensils, shoes and some types of clothing for villagers were located in the cities. Walled cities were also places of refuge if an enemy army appeared in the land. Again, a city could settle disputes between village-dwellers, and oversee sales of land. From the religious point of view, sanctuaries were located in cities and were thus resorted to when villagers needed to make either voluntary offerings or those stipulated by their religious commitments.

The Song of Songs can be read in many ways and at many levels, but one way of approaching its poems is by assuming that it represents the point of view of a young woman whose relationship with a young man is circumscribed by the conventions that exist and can be enforced in the city. The countryside, on the other hand is seen as the place where love between a young man and young woman can be expressed joyfully and without restrictions and inhibitions. No doubt these points of view are idealizations. It could also be said that the conventions and restrictions that are maintained in the city are there to protect young women from unscrupulous men. Whether the young women would agree is another matter. We may have something not unlike the many conflicts played out in today's world between teenage girls who resent the restrictions placed upon them by their parents, and parents who argue, rightly or wrongly, that they are acting in the best interests of their offspring.

Probably the most heart-rending expression of the young woman's frustration is found in Song of Songs 8:1–2.

> O that you were like a brother to me,
> that nursed at my mother's breast!
> If I met you outside, I would kiss you,
> and none would despise me.
> I would lead you and bring you into the house of my mother,
> and into the chamber of her that conceived me.
> I would give you spiced wine to drink,
> the juice of my pomegranates.

She regrets that different conventions and rules apply to young men outside the immediate family circle compared with siblings. If she were to meet her brother in the street, nobody would object to her kissing him and inviting him into the house. It would be quite impossible to do these things if he were a young man whom she could marry. Her frustrated longings are further expressed in words that occur elsewhere in Song of Songs, the final verse being something of a refrain:

> O that his left hand were under my head,
> and that his right hand embraced me!
> I adjure you, O daughters of Jerusalem,
> that you stir not up nor awake love
> until it please.
> (Song 8:3–4; compare 2:6–7, 3:5, 5:8)

The wishes of the young woman appear to be fulfilled in an earlier passage:

> I found him whom my soul loves,
> I held him, and would not let him go
> until I had brought him into my mother's house,
> and into the chamber of her that conceived me
> (Song 3:4)

but the context makes it clear that this is either a dream or fantasy:

> Upon my bed by night
> I sought him whom my soul loves;
> I sought him but found him not
> (Song 3:1)

The poem goes on to say that the young woman searched the streets and squares of the city, and sought help from the watchman, and then suddenly came across her lover, whom she then took to her chamber. We must not forget the reality: that Israelite cities were very small, and that even Jerusalem in the fourth or third century BCE, the presumed time of composition of the poem, was no bigger than a very small neighbourhood in a modern city.

A very similar, longer, poem occurs at 5:2–8. Again, it is either a dream or a fantasy, but it expresses not only the frustrations of a young woman in love but also the brutalities of the city directed towards a vulnerable young woman in the city alone at night. In her dream or fantasy, the young woman hears her lover knocking at the door:

> Open to me, my sister, my love,
> my dove, my perfect one;
> for my head is wet with dew,
> my locks with the drops of the night
> (Song 5:2)

The young woman finds that her response is impeded by her nakedness (she needs to dress) and by the need to find footwear. Further, the prospect of seeing her lover is so thrilling that the nervousness it engenders hinders her as she seeks to unbar the door.

> I arose to open to my beloved,
> and my hands dripped with myrrh,
> my fingers with liquid myrrh,
> upon the handles of the bolt. (v.5)

By the time she has opened the door her lover has gone. Whether this is part of the fantasy – a way of expressing unfulfilled desire – or whether readers are entitled to look for more prosaic reasons – the lover is chased off by the watchmen – is left open by the poem. The watchmen enter into the poem, however, as the young woman sets off in search of her lover.

> The watchmen found me,
> as they went about in the city;
> they beat me, they wounded me,
> they took away my mantle,
> those watchmen of the walls. (v.7)

Again, is this fantasy, or is there an underlying truth: the fact that in cities, those appointed to maintain safety can and do abuse the responsibilities that they are given?

Something that may be implicit in this poem is the phenomenon of loneliness in the city. The poem (and its near relative in 3:1–5) contradicts reality in that it seems to portray a young woman living on her own, as might well be the case in a modern city today. But people did not live on their own in ancient cities, and certainly not if they were unmarried young women. (The same is still true in many traditional sub-cultures or societies in the world today.) The woman in the poem of 5:2–8 would hardly in reality be living in a chamber to which her lover could seek access by knocking, and to which she could admit him by opening the door. She would almost certainly be sleeping in a room with her mother and sisters. Yet loneliness can take various forms, and it is possible to be lonely when surrounded by others. The fact that the poem speaks as though the woman is alone is an indication of her inner thoughts and feelings. The poem also hints at the impersonal nature of life in the city. In reality, Israelite cities were sufficiently small for it to be unlikely that anything could happen without everybody knowing. Could the identity of a nocturnal visitor, or the fruitless search of the young woman, or her ill-treatment at the hands of the watchmen be concealed from general knowledge? Yet the poem implies that the answer to these questions is "yes"; and by implying this answer the poem paradoxically indicates that just as there can be loneliness in the midst of a crowd, so things can be impersonal when everything can be known.

The Song of Songs, however else it can be read, is certainly a highly personal account of what it meant for a young woman to live in a city in Old Testament times. Conventions to which lives are expected to conform can be liberating or enslaving, although there are graduated alternatives within these two extremes. The Song of Songs portrays the countryside as liberating and the city as enslaving, from the point of view of a young woman. Although the book contains much by way of idealizing and fantasy, it can also be read as a challenge to city-dwellers today to ask where their perceptions and experience of the city lie within the spectrum between emancipation and enslavement.

The City as the Battleground for Justice and Honesty

Psalm 12 – words, truth and lies
Psalm 12 reads (in my translation)

> 1. Help me, Lord, for God-fearing men are no more,
> and the faithful have vanished from human society.
> 2. People tell lies to each other;
> their speech is smooth but their heart is deceitful.
> 3. Would that the Lord would cut off all smooth speech,
> and tongues that boast so shamelessly,
> 4. that say 'Our speech will win the day,
> we can say what we like.
> Who will restrain us?'
> 5. 'Because the poor are plundered and the destitute groan for help,
> I will rise at once', says the Lord.
> 6. 'I will make them safe from those who trouble them.'
> The words of the Lord are pure,
> like silver and gold refined seven times.
> 7. You will surely guard them, Lord;
> you will protect us from this evil generation for ever.
> 8. The wicked walk confidently on every side
> when what is worthless is esteemed among men.

A recent book entitled *The Greatest Story ever Sold. The Decline and Fall of Truth from 9/11 to Katrina* (Rich, 2006) argues that the administration of President George W. Bush has been characterized by presentations of the "truth" that were at variance with the facts known at the time and certainly with the facts as they have come to be known since. The same story could no doubt also be told in Britain. Certainly, a majority of members of the British Parliament were persuaded in 2003 to join American military action in Iraq, on the grounds that Iraq's dictator, Saddam Hussein, possessed weapons of mass destruction, including weapons that could be directed against Britain at 45 minutes' notice. These claims made in the British parliament not only contradicted the facts as known at the time, but the facts as they have come to be known since.

The feelings of despair that such dishonesty and manipulation of the truth engender in people who have a concern for justice and truth is eloquently expressed in Psalm 12. Parallel to the claim attributed by the psalmist to those who abuse the truth:

> Our speech will win the day,
> we can say what we like.
> Who will restrain us?

is the statement reported by Rich from a Bush administration aide: "when we act, we create our own reality" (Rich, 2006: 3).

The manipulation, and thus the falsification, of the truth leads to a situation where trust in those in authority breaks down completely, and leads to cynicism. Worse than this, it may engender an active selfishness, with the maxim, "if they do not care for truth and honesty, why should I care?"

For the psalmist, complete hopelessness and selfish cynicism are not options because of his belief that God is ultimately the guardian of truth and honesty. "The words of the Lord are pure, like silver and gold refined several times" (v. 6). The very fact that the psalmist complains to God about the abuse of the truth, shows that he does not agree that the wicked who maintain that "we can say what we like" (v. 4) will have the last word.

What has this got to do with the city? As the place where power resides, i.e. which has access to the most important resources and the means of distributing them, the city is where the temptation to abuse power – i.e. to distribute the resources in the interests of those who do the distributing – is at its greatest. Manipulation of the facts, or, to say the same things in other words, the distortion of the truth, is part and parcel of the abuse of power. The psalmist makes it clear that this has practical consequences:

> "Because the poor are plundered
> and the destitute groan for help,
> I will arise at once", says the Lord.

This is not just a matter of the truth for its own sake, important as this is. The abuse of power and the distortion of the truth can have dire consequences for people, especially the poor and destitute. A highly regrettable feature of the Iraq crisis is the unwillingness of the administrations of Britain and the United States to acknowledge how many casualties have been inflicted upon innocent Iraqi citizens by the allied armies. Estimates provided by respected independent agencies are invariably challenged as being exaggerated or based upon flawed methodologies. The fact that the government departments that question the figures are the same departments that confidently asserted that Iraq had weapons of mass destruction and that some could be targeted against

Britain in 45 minutes, would be laughable if it were not for the fact that many thousands of innocent lives have been lost and/or ruined as a result of government "spin". Psalm 12 voices the perplexity of someone in the city who sees the truth being manipulated in the interests of those in power. Psalm 55 is the agonized prayer of someone whose very life is in danger because of those who abuse their power in the city.

Threats to those who seek to maintain integrity in the city
Psalm 55 (my translation)
After his opening plea to God the psalmist describes his predicament:

> I am distressed at the voice of the enemy,
> at the onslaught of the wicked,
> for they heap wickedness upon me
> and are vindictive in their anger. (v. 3)

He wishes that he could go elsewhere, so as to be free from the predicament:

> O that I had the wings of a dove;
> I would fly away and find rest.
> I would escape far away,
> and find refuge in the wilderness. (vv. 6–7)

What the circumstances are, are described in verses 9–11:

> I have seen violence and contention in the city.
> Day and night they compass the city on its walls,
> and wickedness and trouble are within it.
> Destruction is in its midst,
> and oppression and deceit are never absent from its square.

While it is not always advisable to turn poetry into prose, these lines need to be read in the light of what was said in the first chapter about the archaeology of Israelite cities. The phrase "they [the wicked] compass the city on its walls" conveys the sense of a total grip on power on the part of the wicked, just as the walls entirely surround the city. The phrase "oppression and deceit are never absent from the square" has to be read in the light of the function of the square. It was the main, and often only, public space in the city. It was where trade was carried on, and where justice was administered. The phrase thus conveys the sense of dishonest trading and the perversion of justice, two activities not completely divorced from each other.

The psalm continues with a brief personal note to the effect that the wickedness is not being carried out by people who have always been at enmity with the psalmist, but by one (or perhaps those) who was/were once a companion and friend. The implication is that the psalmist's attempt to hold on to what is honest and true has led him into enmity with friends who have allowed themselves to become corrupt and unprincipled. Some verses later (v. 20) the psalmist complains that:

> They lay violent hands on those who belong to God;
> they profane his covenant.

Surrounded by these troubles the psalmist remains confident that the wicked will ultimately not have the last word. For if the city is a place where the powers of wickedness can come together to produce evil that is greater than the sum of the parts, it is also a place where hope and action sustained by prayer can deny that this evil is the only reality.

The city as the place of wickedness justified by unjust laws: Psalm 94
Perhaps the most powerful description of the city as the arena of wickedness and injustice comes in Psalm 94. Not only is the language vividly descriptive; two factors are added which were not explicit in Psalms 12 and 55. These are the passing of unjust laws, and the use of religion to cover up the true state of affairs. These last two points are expressed in verse 20 (my translation throughout the psalm):

> Can those who cover up their wickedness have you [i.e. God] as an ally,
> those who produce evil by passing laws?

The psalmist clearly indicates that the wicked he is indicting are those rulers in the city with the power to legislate. They produce evil by passing laws. They also seem to be, as is common in so many times and places, in close alliance with a religious establishment that serves to justify their rule and their actions. They presume that they have God as their ally.

The true state of affairs is described graphically in earlier verses.

> They murder the widows and strangers,
> and put the fatherless to death. (v. 6)

This is no mere attack against fellow human beings; it has a divine dimension:

> They crush your people, Lord,
> and oppress the ones you have chosen. (v. 8)

The widows, strangers and fatherless belong to God. They are his people. The wicked do what they do because they have acquired a self-confidence that allows them to

> spout forth arrogant words;
> the evil-doers boast proudly. (v. 4)

Compounding all this is an attitude of arrogance towards God that shocks the psalmist:

> They say "Yah will not see.
> The God of Jacob will not notice", (v. 7)

In this dire situation the psalmist gains hope first of all from an intellectual argument based upon his religious faith:

> Cannot he who planted the ear hear?
> Cannot he who formed the eye see?
> Will not he who guides the nations punish them?
> Is the teacher of mankind ignorant? (vv. 9–10)

Using the Hebrew word *hevel*, which also occurs in Ecclesiastes and is usually translated there as "vanity" (cp. Eccl. 1:3, 14) the psalmist compares the arrogance of the wicked with their nothingness in comparison with God:

> The LORD knows the thoughts of man,
> that they are wind. [Hebr. *Hevel*] (v. 11)

However, the faith of the psalmist is not only intellectual, but something that sustains him as he seeks to oppose the wicked.

> Who will stand up for me against the wicked?
> Who will stand by me against evil-doers?
> If the LORD had not been my helper
> I would soon have been put to silence.
> But when I said "My foot has slipped",
> your unfailing love, LORD, held me up. (vv. 16–17)

Further, the psalmist's hope in the triumph of God's justice lets a glimmer of light enter into an otherwise dark psalm, and enables the city to be glimpsed as a symbol of hope:

> For the LORD will not forsake his people,
> nor abandon those he has chosen.
> For justice will once more be administered rightly,
> and all who are true of heart will be glad. (vv. 14–15)

The statement that "justice will once more be administered rightly" points to the city at its best, as a place where people will come to trust each other as they see justice being exercised in the interests of the truth, and not in the interests of those who have power.

The City as an Indication of the Horrors of War: Lamentations

Because cities are where power is concentrated and where the powerful reside, they have always been the chief targets in warfare. This is as true today as it was in the ancient world. No one aims to drop bombs today in the middle of a desert or open countryside. Bombs are dropped on cities, with the aim of destroying their industrial capacity and their communication centres. In the ancient world cities were targeted not only because they accommodated the ruling classes and controlled important resources; to possess a city enabled an invading ruler to claim authority over the area of which the city was the capital, regardless of whether that area was occupied or in any way controlled by the invading army.

War was not as brutal in the ancient world as it has become in modern times, but it was bad enough, and the book of Lamentations is a vivid description of war and its aftermath. Recent scholarship has dated its final form to the fourth century BCE, and this is an important finding. Whereas earlier critical scholarship dated it to the sixth century and suggested that the book's material originated in corporate laments that took place in the ruins of Jerusalem after 587, the later dating has advantages. While not denying that some of the laments in Lamentations may derive from actual mourning ceremonies, the later date enables the book to be seen as a warning – a warning to later generations about the horrors of war, in the hope that they might be avoided in future.

Before the descriptions of the plight of the ruined city are considered, it must be emphasized that Lamentations is primarily a remarkable theological composition. It attributes the destruction that overtook the city to the action of God in judging the people; and it nowhere suggests that this punishment was other than fully deserved. The book contains two verses that have inspired modern hymns:

> The steadfast love of the LORD never ceases,
> his mercies never come to an end;
> they are new every morning;
> great is thy faithfulness. (Lam. 3:22–3)

These verses are part of the hope that the book contains, that God's sovereign power is able to restore the city that has been destroyed.

If, however, attention is turned to the description of the plight of the people in the aftermath of the destruction, the most poignant passage can be found in 5:3–4, 8–15:

> We have become orphans, fatherless;
> our mothers are like widows.

We must pay for the water we drink,
the wood we get must be bought.
With a yoke on our necks we are hard driven;
we are weary, we are given no rest.
Slaves rule over us;
there is none to deliver us from their hand.
We get our bread at the peril of our lives,
because of the sword in the wilderness.
Our skin is hot as an oven
with the burning heat of famine.
Women are ravished in Zion,
virgins in the towns of Judah.
Princes are hung up by their hands;
no respect is shown to the elders.
Young men are compelled to grind at the mill;
and boys stagger under loads of wood.
The old men have quit the city gate,
the young men their music.
The joy of our hearts has ceased;
our dancing has been turned to mourning.

These verses make it possible for the situation in the ruined city to be reconstructed with reasonable certainty. There is an absence of men of fighting age. Their death in the fighting or their exile and imprisonment means that children have become, in practice, fatherless, and their mothers have become widows (5:3). Men are not entirely absent, of course, but it is notable that the passage mentions only young men and boys, and old men (5:13–14). In the ruined city, which also has to support an occupying garrison, the public amenities such as supplies of water and wood are administered by the occupying power. It is possible that verse 4, which states that water and wood must be bought, refers not to a general charge for these things levied by the occupiers, but to the bribery which they both encourage and turn a blind eye to, a system that enables those who have things with which to barter to get more than their fair share of the resources.

Public amenities are not the only things to have come under the direction of the occupiers. Those who can work, and this will be predominantly the women, are organized into labour gangs, perhaps to rebuild the buildings occupied by the garrison, to remove and bury the corpses of humans and animals, and to clear up the rubble from ruined walls and houses. Verse 5, which speaks of the people as having a yoke on their neck, aptly describes this forced labour.

In verse 8 the complaint is that slaves rule over the people. If these are slaves who formerly served masters in the city, this is an unpleasant reversal of fortunes for the free citizens. An occupying power could well see in slaves a useful source of overseers who would be loyal to them rather than their former masters. It may also be that the "slaves" are part of the garrison, but who are regarded by the free citizens as belonging to a slave class. The breakdown of normal relationships and the desperation for survival spread from the city to the surrounding countryside which supplies the city with its food. Verse 9 describes a situation in which a kind of anarchy makes the production of food an uncertain and dangerous business. The resulting shortage of food weakens the resistance of the population to illnesses such as fever (verse 10). Women are always especially vulnerable to the predatory sexual desires of invading armies, and Jerusalem and the cities of Judah are no exception (verse 11). Nobles and elders who took temporary refuge in the countryside when the city was besieged and who now return (cp. Jer. 40:11–12), do not escape punishment (verse 12). The young men and boys who are made to turn the mill-stones and to carry huge loads of wood may either be doing work normally carried out by animals such as donkeys, or work carried out by slaves (verse 13). The city gate, the centre of the legal, administrative and social life of the city is deserted (verse 14). There is no occasion for music or celebration.

One group of innocent sufferers not mentioned in 5:1–15 is young children and infants. Their plight is touched upon in earlier chapters. A poet writing in the first person describes his overwhelming grief:

> because infants and babes faint in the streets of the city.
> They cry to their mothers, "where is bread and wine?";
> as they faint like wounded men in the streets of the city,
> as their life is poured out on their mothers' bosom. (Lam. 2:11–12)

Another poem describes how

> the tongue of the nursling cleaves to the roof of its mouth for thirst;
> the children beg for food, but no one gives to them. (4:4)

As if this were not bad enough, another passage speaks of the dilemma of compassionate mothers who, in order to secure their survival and presumably that of their other infants, are reduced to cannibalism:

> The hands of compassionate women have boiled their own children,
> they became food in the destruction of the daughter of my people. (4:10)

No wonder the poet reflects that

> Happier were the victims of the sword
> than the victims of hunger,

who pined away, stricken
by want of the fruits of the field. (4:8)

The need for compassionate mothers to use their own children for food is
an indication of how the most deeply embedded moral and emotional
feelings are subverted by war and its aftermath. As the poet remarks: "Even
the jackals give the breast and suckle their young" (4:3), but war subverts
everything so that even the most precious things, human lives, are regarded
as worthless. The poet makes this last point by likening the inhabitants of
Jerusalem to gold and precious stones that have been scattered in the streets:

How the gold has grown dim,
how the pure gold is changed!
The holy stones lie scattered
at the head of every street.
The precious sons of Zion,
worth their weight in gold,
how they are reckoned as earthen pots,
the work of a potter's hands! (4:1–2)

It was noted earlier in this section that Lamentations is a theological work
that ascribes the plight of the city to God's just punishment. Modern readers
would probably want to put things rather differently. Lamentations is a
vivid description of what happens when humans act inhumanly against
each other. If God is involved, it is not because he wills the devastation and
degradation nor because he uses human agencies to bring them about. It is
rather that God is involved by being rejected by those by those who unleash
war and its consequences. Some wars, of course, are necessary as lesser evils,
and those who instigate them have not necessarily rejected God. They are,
however, having to respond to a situation in which the rejection of God by
others makes it necessary to wage war as a lesser evil. The city is the lens, so
to speak, that magnifies the enormities of inhumanity and makes it possible
to see them in their starkest reality.

The City as a Symbol of Universal Peace and Justice: Micah 4:1–4

The poem found at Micah 4:1–4 is also found in an almost identical version
in Isaiah 2:2–4, the main difference being the lack of Micah 4:4 in the
Isaiah text. Although the Micah version is generally held to provide a
more accurate text of the poem, it was certainly not composed or spoken by
Micah. It was added by the compilers of his book in order to soften the
biting criticisms of Jerusalem found in Micah 3:1–7 which culminate in
the declaration in 3:12 that Jerusalem will be destroyed and not rebuilt.

The poem was probably not composed or said by the eighth century prophet Isaiah either but, like the Micah passage, was most likely added by editors of the book to soften the criticism of Jerusalem in Isaiah 1. However, the fact that the poem appears in two prophetic books is an indication of its importance. Scholars have pointed to similarities between some of the phrases in the poem, and material elsewhere in the Old Testament, especially Joel 4:10 where, in the context of a summons to war, the hearers are exhorted to:

> Beat your ploughshares into swords,
> and your pruning hooks into spears.

Whether Micah 4:3

> they shall beat their swords into ploughshares,
> and their spears into pruning hooks

is a deliberate reversal of Joel 4:10 or vice versa, it is clear that a saying about swords and spears, and ploughshares and pruning hooks was well known among the people.

Cities as places to which people go for special occasions have always been a feature of life, and this is still the case. In today's world cities are the venue for concerts, plays, operas, sporting events, exhibitions and prestigious shops and restaurants. Railways have their termini in cities, not to mention major airports on their outskirts. Ancient cities did not offer quite as many attractions, except that Graeco-Roman foundations could offer theatres and sporting arenas for chariot races and gladiatorial combats. In ancient Israel Jerusalem became a city of pilgrimage, to which a parallel might be the pilgrimage to Canterbury made famous in Geoffrey Chaucer's *Canterbury Tales*, or that to Compostella in Spain. Old Testament religious laws required all Israelite males to appear before God three times at the central sanctuary (cp. Deut. 16:16), and whether or not this was actually observed when the poem in Micah 4:1–4 was composed (in the fourth century BCE?), the practice of pilgrimage provides the image, central to the poem, of people streaming up to Jerusalem.

The poem begins by envisaging a transformation of the natural state of affairs. Jerusalem is by no means built on the highest mountain in its vicinity. It is, in fact, overlooked, particularly by the hills on its eastern side. It became the site of a city because it, alone, possessed a permanent supply of water from the spring called Gihon. The poem foresees the physical exaltation of Jerusalem above other mountains, a poetic way of emphasizing not only its importance, but that what is to happen will be caused by God.

In response to this action, nations will be moved to go to Jerusalem. However, unlike the bargain-seekers today who flock to the sales in the cities just after Christmas, the nations are drawn to Jerusalem not by the desire for selfish gain, but by a desire for something that will make humans more human and lead to peace and justice:

> Come, let us go up to the mountain of the LORD ...
> that he may teach us his ways
> and we may walk in his paths. (Mic. 4:2)

The judgements that will be made by God between the nations (4:3) will be so profoundly fair, convincing and moving, that the nations themselves will desire not to learn war any more. The famous passage about beating swords into ploughshares is profoundly significant. Wars consume vast amounts of natural resources. The present writer can still vividly remember the day during his childhood in South London in the Second World War when the cast-iron railings that surrounded playing fields and stood on top of many garden walls of houses were taken away, never to be replaced. They were melted down to provide the raw materials for armaments. During the First World War, the remains of the ancient pine forests in the Coastal Plain of Palestine were cut down by the Turks and used to fuel the railways. At the end of wars it is not only the defeated who face hardship. Victors also have to pay the price, especially when the use of raw materials to produce armaments leads to a shortage of essential things once the emergency is over. Beating swords into ploughshares implies a massive change in human outlook and practice. It implies a different world – a better world; one symbolized by the city as a place where nations learn and long to live in peace.

Chapter 3

MAKING CONNECTIONS

In his *Minima Moralia* T. W. Adorno wrote as follows:

> There is nothing innocuous left. The little pleasures, expressions of life that seemed exempt from the responsibility of thought, not only have an element of defiant silliness, of callous refusal to see, but directly serve their diametrical opposite. Even the blossoming tree lies the moment its bloom is seen without the shadow of terror; even the innocent "How lovely!" becomes an excuse for an existence outrageously unlovely, and there is no longer beauty or consolation except in the gaze falling on horror, withstanding it, and in unalleviated consciousness of negativity holding fast to the possibility of what is better. (Adorno, 1997: 26; E.T.: 25)

What Adorno meant by this is that humans spend much of their time deceiving themselves about the true nature of the world in which they live. The tree loaded with blossom in spring can help to perpetuate this self-delusion if it engenders a feeling that all is well with the world, whereas the reality is that the blossoming tree is part of a world characterized as much by terror and evil as by beautiful phenomena of nature. According to Adorno the only way to appreciate or conceive of beauty in today's world is to look its terrors and evils in the face and to imagine what the world might be like if they were transformed into something better.

Adorno's observation is a helpful way in to what the Old Testament says about the city. Much of what it contains on this subject is negative. The founders of the first city (Genesis 4) are murderers. The city, built by slave labour, is a symbol of the desire of the powerful to run the world in opposition to the justice of God (Genesis 11). It is a place where resources are accumulated by the powerful and where those in need are disregarded (the verdict on Sodom in Ezekiel 16:46–9). It is a place of loneliness and frustration in the midst of crowds (Song 5), a place where truth and justice are corrupted in the interests of those in power (Pss 12, 55 and 94). As the principal target in time of war the city is a lens which magnifies the horrors of human inhumanity to other humans (Lamentations). The Old

Testament does not try to conceal or cover up these realities. Where it has a vision of hope, as in Micah 4:1–4, this comes from imagining a transformation of the horrors so boldly described elsewhere: nations do not go up against the city to make war, but to learn peace. They ally themselves together not for the purposes of doing evil but to learn what is good. The weapons of war are deployed not in order to kill and main, but are re-forged in order to produce food that will benefit everyone.

The danger against which Adorno warns is of a complacency that tries to shut out the dark realities of life, to look away from the shadows cast by injustice and wickedness. That temptation will be strongest today for those who live in leafy suburbs and who get to other parts of the city by driving along dual carriageways flanked by trees and with central areas planted with flowers. Those who live in suburbs will have no reason or desire to venture by foot into parts of the city where the ugly sides of life are not so easily hidden or obscured. The present writer remembers vividly the grim housing estates in the parts of south London where he grew up, and the appalling slums of Moss Side in the Manchester of the late 1950s when he was a student.

It is not necessary to turn to the Old Testament to learn about the evils that have and do beset life in cities. In the nineteenth century Charles Dickens sought to combat these evils by making them the themes of some of his novels and in the twentieth century Bertold Brecht used drama as a way of social critique. What has been attempted in the previous pages has been to help readers see the city from an Old Testament perspective; perhaps, to read the Bible in a way that they have not previously done, or thought was possible. The Old Testament remains a foundation document of faith for Christians and Jews (for whom it is not an *old* testament), communities that are committed in their different ways to the kingdom of God – to an order of right relationships, truth, peace and justice. For Christians, the New Testament adds a further dimension to this commitment, a dimension that will occupy the second part of this book. The Old Testament can also be read as complete in itself on the matter of the city, with its realistic portrayals of its dilemmas and its hopes centred upon the visions that come from God. Towards the end of his *Minima Moralia* Adorno observes that:

> Perspectives must be fashioned that displace and estrange the world, reveal it to be, with its rifts and crevices, as indigent and distorted as it will appear one day in the messianic light. (Adorno: 283/203/233. E.T.: 247)

This is arguably what the Old Testament does in its portrayals of the city, thereby issuing a call for creative thought and action.

BIBLIOGRAPHY

Adorno, T. W. 1978. *Minima Moralia. Reflexionen aus dem beschädigten Leben,* Gesammelte Schriften Band 4. Frankfurt a. M: Suhrkamp Taschenbuch 1997; Darmstadt: Wissenschaftliche Buchgesellschaft, ET; London: Verso.

Bourdieu, P. 1977. *Outline of a Theory of Practice.* Cambridge: Cambridge University Press.

Broshi, M. and R. Gophna. 1986. "Middle Bronze Age II Palestine: Its Settlements and Population". *Bulletin of the American Schools of Oriental Research,* 261, 73–90.

De Geus, C. H. J. 2003. *Towns in Ancient Israel and in the Southern Levant* (Palaestina Antiqua 10). Leuven: Peeters.

Fritz, V. 1990. *Die Stadt im alten Israel.* Munich: C. H. Beck.

Giddens, A. 1992. *Human Societies. An Introductory Reader in Sociology.* Cambridge: Polity Press.

Grabbe, L. L. 2004. *A History of the Jews and Judaism in the Second Temple Period. Volume 1. Yehud: A History of the Persian Province of Judah.* London: T. & T. Clark International.

Gray, J. 1964. *I & II Kings* (Old Testament Library). London: SCM Press.

King, P. J. and L. E. Stager. 2001. *Life in Biblical Israel.* Louisville, KT: Westminster John Knox.

McKane, W. 1970. *Proverbs.* Philadelphia, PA: Westminster Press, Old Testament Library.

Müller, H.-P., O. Kaiser and J. A. Loader. 1992. *Das Hohelied, Klagelieder, Das Buch Esther* (Das Alte Deutsch 16/2). Göttingen: Vandenhoeck & Ruprecht.

Noth, M. 1965. *Leviticus* (Old Testament Library). London: SCM Press.

Otto, E. 1980. *Jerusalem – die Geschichte der Heiligen Stadt.* Stuttgart: W. Kohlhammer.

Overy, R. 1997. *Russia's War.* London: Penguin Books.

Pacione, M. 1992. "Major Trends in World Urbanization". In A. Giddens, *Human Societies. An Introductory Reader in Sociology.* Cambridge: Polity Press, pp. 294–7.

Rad, G. von. 1961. "Die Stadt auf dem Berge". In C. Levin, *Gesammelte Studien zum Alten Testament.* Munich: Chr. Kaiser, pp. 214–24.

Rich, F. 2006. *The Greatest Story ever Sold. The Decline and Fall of Truth from 9/11 to Katrina.* New York: Penguin Press.

Rogerson, J. W. 1991. *Genesis 1–11* (Old Testament Guides). Sheffield: Sheffield Academic Press.

Rogerson, J. W. and P. R. Davies. 2005. *The Old Testament World* (2nd edition). Louisville, KT: Westminster John Knox; London: T. & T. Clark International.
Westermann, C. 1970. *Genesis* (Biblischer Kommentar Altes Testament I, 5). Neukirchen-Vluyn: Neukirchener Verlag.

Part 2

THE CITY IN THE NEW TESTAMENT

John Vincent

Chapter 4

INTRODUCTION: THE POLITICAL SITUATION

By the time of the first century, the whole of Palestine, like the whole of the eastern end of the Mediterranean, was part of the Roman Empire. Everywhere, Rome imposed its control over areas, by the erection of major cities, often with fortresses and citadels, with their characteristic streets and public places, their forums, theatres, temples and great houses. All these were in some cases introduced into existing local towns, in other cases built on "green" sites.

But alongside those Roman cities, many local indigenous villages, towns and even cities already existed, and were allowed to remain. Yet these locations were never "pure" or arcane or rustic. Most had already received in various ways the imprints of previous occupying nations and their varied cultures. Most Palestinian residential areas would already have had imposed upon them, or been willing absorbents for, elements from pre-Roman occupying forces – Persian (450–332 BCE), Greek (332–167), Seleucid/Syrian (197–37), and then Roman (37 BCE –132 CE). There were also the periods of the Maccabean rulers (166–63), and the Herodians (37 BCE –70 CE). Palestine in the first century bore the marks of influences and buildings from all these sources (Harding, 2003: 5–55).

Rome, in fact, was able to take over and centralize the Hellenistic urban scene which already permeated all aspects of society.

> At the centre of it was the concept of the *polis* with its organised, polished, economic, administrative, as well as philosophical and social implications. It was a fundamental concept which was to spread to all lands and peoples who were touched by Greek culture, even to Rome itself (Pliny in the first century uses the word *civitas* to describe such communities). The resulting Hellenism, i.e. Greek language, produced a cosmopolitan fraternity which vaulted the narrow bounds of mere race or nationality. (Browning, 1982: 63)

The Roman cities were places of power and influence, but also places from which the surrounding villages and small towns could be controlled. The small towns might have their own outpost of soldiers, but were otherwise controlled by co-operating locals, including Herod and the tax-collectors of the gospels.

However, the way that the Old Testament addresses those in power in the cities, described by John Rogerson in the first part of this book, has now disappeared. The people in power in the cities of New Testament times plainly were not Israelites, and certainly never Christians. The prophetic denunciations of the unjust rulers in the Old Testament have their origin in the fact that those rulers were members of the people of God. Their unjust behaviour was a violation of their duties to care for their fellow religionists. The city as 'an institution ..., justly and rightly governed in obedience to God' (p. 4, above) simply no longer existed, as fellow Israelites no longer held power. Those that held some elements of power, like the Herods, the Sadducees and the high priests, could not be expected to carry out Torah's demands for justice to fellow Israelites if or when that would undermine the support of Rome, which alone legitimized their position.

Thus, there is no continuation of the Old Testament images of the city as "the symbol of Human Rebellion against God", as in Babel, or as "the city of Wrong", as in Sodom (cf. above, pp. 24–27). Nor yet is there anything like the lyrical urban scene of the Song of Songs (above, pp. 27–31), or the city itself as "the battleground for justice and honesty" (pp. 31–34) or as "a symbol of universal peace and justice" (pp. 39–41).

Not only, as John Rogerson says, can the Old Testament "be read as complete in itself on the matter of the city" (p. 43). It also does not have as its logical successor (except to Christian eyes) the New Testament. The historical and logical successors to the Old Testament are the writings which came from the same sources between the probable date of the last of the Old Testament writings – Micah in the fourth century BCE (p. 40) or Lamentations in the fourth century BCE (p. 36) – and four centuries later, when New Testament writings emerged – Paul first, in the 40s CE. These writings are those now known to us as the Apocrypha, which originate between the Second Temple in 515 BCE and the Fall of Jerusalem in 70 CE (Harding, 2003: 56–108, 130–74).

Two decisive factors came between our two Testaments. First, the whole country was subject to total domination by a succession of foreign powers, as we have seen. The result of this was that the city, and especially the holy city of Jerusalem, became a pawn in the hands of alien oppressors, with its Temple and its worship only surviving when the occupying power allowed it – and on variable terms. Thus, "the city" could only with widely ranging degrees of truth continue its religious role.

The second factor is a decisive consequence of this. Jerusalem became less and less an image of present God-centred reality, and more and more an image of a desperately hoped-for future when Jerusalem would be liberated from foreign bondage and reasserted as the home of Israel's God and Israel's people. Jerusalem, the Holy City, the city set on a hill, to which even the foreigners will come, became only a future, ideal image. As such, it is familiar in Apocalyptic writings (Harding, 2003: 130–43), and in Revelation.

In the New Testament, the focus is no longer upon the general life of people and their history, with occasional national events and heroic individuals, as in the Old Testament. The New Testament does not concern itself with a nation or its cities existing at least in principle under the sovereignty and authority of a God. Rather, the cities are the urban spaces essentially under the control of those of whom, and for whom, the books were not written, and by whom the marginal and very particular stories were neither read nor known about.

The story of the figure who becomes "Good News" to others is that of a person of no significance in the urban history of the time, whose "notices" in secular sources are scant and not even contemporary, and whose existence and activity in the villages and cities of Galilee passed totally without comment by the citizens, Roman or Judaistic, of the time. Likewise, the tales of otherwise totally unknown individuals like Paul and Peter are told against the backdrop of and within the circumstances of great Roman urban centres. But the politics, government, laws, customs and policies of those centres were nowhere of direct interest to the marginal, fledgling Christian groups, save when they impinged upon the activities of the tiny "Good News" groups who came and went largely unnoticed.

It is therefore not possible with the New Testament writings to describe incidents or circumstances in which the life of the cities is *as such* a matter of concern.

Yet the tiny Gospel groups in Galilee and the Empire did presume to be concerned with what the powerful were doing – but in a very special way, related to their practice of seeking to celebrate and extend the presence on earth of the Kingdom of God, announced and embodied by Jesus (Mk 1:14) but only present in the world to the Gospel-informed eye which might discern its secret presence.

With these general thoughts in mind, we turn to consider what can be known about the two decisive areas of Jesus's activity, Galilee and Jerusalem – and then to take ourselves to the wider world of Paul and the first Christians.

Chapter 5

The City and the World of Jesus

Jesus and Galilee

In the last 20 years, increasing archaeological evidence from Galilee suggests that the old picture of it as an almost totally rural culture was incorrect. Twenty-five years ago Wayne Meeks had observed that "within a decade of the crucifixion of Jesus, the village culture of Palestine had been left behind, and the Greco-Roman city became the dominant environment of the Christian movement" (Meeks, 1983: 11).

More recent studies by Reed (2000), Sawicki (2000), Crossan and Reed (2001), Moxnes (2003), Thiede (2004) and Freyne (2008) describe elements of urban life throughout Galilee. A careful reading of the works just cited will reveal differences between them, but the picture emerging is very plain: the peaceful, idyllic Galilean countryside was penetrated by many aspects of urban life, and was subject to them in many ways. The urban intertwines with the rural, just as the Roman and Hellenistic intertwine with the Judaistic.

Sawicki asks the question: "What are the signs of 'Jewishness' in Galilee? What does 'Jewish space' look like?" She answers:

> For archaeology these are scientific questions, and they are not easy to answer satisfactorily. On one hand, inscribed Hebrew letters and decorative motifs such as the menorah bespeak the intention of ancient builders to construct and furnish a place "Jewishly", to house aspects of an intentionally Jewish way of life. On the other hand, in the Roman period in Galilee many Jews wrote Greek or Aramaic, used Hellenized names, and behaved "Jewishly" in places adorned with secular and heathen cultural themes, places built with colonial interests in mind. (Sawicki, 2000: 88; cf. Thiede, 2004: 53–73)

Thus, we find a burial description recording a Roman's service to the Jewish community. And there are Jewish features and emblems in otherwise Roman buildings. There were neither Jewish "ghettos" nor purely Roman cities.

Town business was done by elected elders and others in the town meeting, the "gathering" or "bringing together" – Greek *synagogue*, which also served as a place for study and for reading the law. Acts 6:9 names synagogues of freed slaves, of Cyrenians, Alexandrians and Cilesians. There was also a "place of prayer", *proseuche*, in Diaspora Judaism like Philippi (Acts 16:11–15), as well as Galilee. Judea's principal house of justice was the "assembly" or "sitting together" – Greek *synedrion*. The Gospels record it as including Sadducees, Pharisees, and Priests.

During the lifetime of Jesus, the Roman domination of Galilee and Judea became more and more evident. After Herod the Great (37 BCE – 4 CE), Rome imposed four "Tetrarchies". Herod Antipas governed Galilee and Perea (4–39 CE), Philip ruled Trachonitus and Iturea (4 BCE –33 CE), while Judea was governed by Archelaus (4–6 CE) and then as a Roman Province with a Governor or Prefect, including Pontius Pilate (26–36 CE). Sawicki observes:

> Roman power was projected onto Galilee, through the client ruler Herod Antipas, by cultivating indigenous collaborators, by manipulating the economy to draw off commodities and other resources for Roman projects, by relocating families from villages to urban areas, by occasional military incursions, and by diverting international travellers to the new tourist attractions at Tiberias after 20 CE. Economically, it was not the case that "Before urbanization" there was a "surplus" of produce and industrial production just lying around in barns and warehouses of Galilee. ... Surplus had to be created through reorganization of labor, that entailed an upheaval of residence and kinship patterns. The establishment of cities required massive labor displacements, first toward Sepphoris during Jesus' childhood, then to lakeside Tiberias when he was a young man. (Sawicki, 2000: 92)

Evidence is lacking for significant numbers of non-Jews at Sepphoris or Tiberias, either Roman, Greek or Syrophoenician, in the time of Jesus, especially when compared to the evidence at urban sites along the coast or in the Decapolis.

While Sepphoris and Tiberias were Jewish cities that had been more Hellenized than the rest of Galilee, Jesus' activities in and around the more humble Jewish village of Capernaum ironically put him in closer proximity to Gentiles and pagan cities. Still clearly within a Jewish orbit among the Jewish villages on the northwestern shore of the Sea of Galilee, and with the same in portions of the Golan, the Gospels portray Jesus' ministry as taking place on the geographical and cultural fringe. There, he was surrounded by Greeks and other Gentiles living in the Decapolis, as well as by Syro-phoenicians in the Huleh Valley and toward Caesarea Philippi (Reed 2000: 217–218).

All this means that, like all of the Roman Empire, Jesus's Galilee was multicultural. Four miles from Nazareth was the Romans' regional capital city of Sepphoris, built in 15–39 CE by Herod Antipas, one of the three sons of Herod the Great. Sepphoris had government personnel, plus craftsmen, and an entertainment industry to staff the 1,000-seat amphitheatre (Batey, 1991; Reed, 2000: 100–38).

The major Roman Cities of Jesus's time were Sepphoris, Tiberius and Gaba in Galilee, Caesarea Philippi, Hippus, Gadara and Abila beyond Jordan, Ptolemais, Dora, Caesarea, Apollonia, Joppa, Jamnia, Ascalon and Gaza in the coastal region, plus Samaria, Scythopolis, Antipatris, Lydda, Emmaus and Jerusalem in Judea. Archaeology reveals a rich tapestry of forum, basilica, amphitheatre, market, bath house, public buildings, roads, city walls, water supply, sewage and drainage (Sperber, 1998). *Ephebate* or gymnasiums were absent, as viciously opposed by Jews, as in the Maccabean revolt (1 Maccabees 1–14; 2 Maccabees 4: 9–14).

Other Old Testament features (see pp. 7–9) continue, such as:

1. The city walls are evident in the larger settlements. The possibility of a house being part of the wall is raised by Acts 9:25.
2. The city gate. This is referred to in Luke 7:12, 16:20 (house), Acts 3:2, 10; 9:24; 10:17; 12:10, 14; 14:13.
3. The houses. The picture of "two storeys possibly topped by an upper room as a third storey' (p. 10) would fit with the house whose roof is uncovered (Mk 2:4), or perhaps the "large upper room" of Mark 14:15 or Acts 1:13.
4. Water. The dependence of cities on wells and tunnels within the city (pp. 13–14) was clearly supplanted in New Testament times by bringing large supplies of water across the country by way of aqueducts, though reference to these in the New Testament is lacking.
5. Craftsmen. It is disputed as to how far the description of Jesus in Mark 6:3 as *tekton* indicates a specific craft of house builder or carpenter, and how far it merely indicates a "jobbing builder", or a hired worker.

Galilee was a productive area. Josephus, its one-time Governor (*c.* 37–93 CE), describes Galilee thus:

> The land is everywhere so rich in soil and pasturage and produces such a variety of trees that even the most indolent are tempted by these facilities to engage in agriculture. In fact it has all been cultivated by the inhabitants and there is not a single portion left waste. The cities too are plentiful and because of the richness of the soil the villages everywhere are so densely populated

that even the smallest of them has a population of over 15,000 inhabitants. (Josephus, 1981: 192)

Nazareth's soil is semi-permeable chalk and marl, with cisterns storing water for the Nazareth ridge, which was intensely terraced and irrigated. The village's probably 30,000 square metres and perhaps 2,000 inhabitants produced grain, vegetables and fruit, and supported livestock. The village craftsmen (*tekton*) like Joseph and Jesus (Mk 6:3, Mt. 13:55) might have supplemented their craftsman's income with the produce of a family field. Jonathan Reed comments:

> For the most part, peasants and their families sought to produce what they consumed and hoped to pass on the required taxes in kind from their surplus, without cutting into their sustenance. (Reed, 2000: 67)

Outside Galilee, Greek culture and political control had established the ten great cities – the Decapolis, which controlled the area in Transjordan from Moab to Damascus (Hammond, 1980).

Judeans resisted Roman intrusions if they could. Pilate had to abandon bringing his cohorts' standards into Jerusalem (*Ant.*18.55), or sacred family shields (Philo, *Legat* 299). Gaias withdrew a plan for his statue to go into the Temple (*Ant.*18.261; *Legat* 203).

How, then, does the Judean/Jewish settlement survive and co-exist with the Roman one? We can answer: with difficulty, and with endless negotiation and modification. A recent planning theorist, Leonie Sandercock, comments:

> "Culture" cannot be understood as static, eternally given, essentialist. It is always evolving, dynamic and hybrid of necessity. All cultures, even allegedly conservative or traditional ones, contain multiple differences within themselves that are continually being re-negotiated. (Sandercock, 2003: 10)

In fact, Sandercock argues for "Mongrel Cities" – cities which integrate immigrants, and develop something greater than the separate cultures contribute individually. The idea of a "mongrel city" would suit Jerusalem and the urban centres of Jesus's day. However much Roman or Hellenistic culture was being imposed on them, the native Judean or Galilean still had to negotiate the terms of it.

We might compare the British experience today. Contemporary Britain is much involved in the debate concerning multiculturalism. Can the British celebrate the cultures of others in their midst? Can the British adjust themselves to not being the dominant culture? How do different cultures contribute to the total culture?

Cities, Towns and Villages

Palestine in the time of Jesus probably had around 2.5 to 3 million people, of whom between 55,000 and 90,000 have been estimated as living in Jerusalem. Josephus puts the number at 3 million in Jerusalem, and the Talmud 12 million, but these figures are unlikely.

A variety of terms indicate gradations in the sizes of the human communities. We confine ourselves to the six terms in Mark's Gospel, many of the texts for which recur in Luke and Matthew.

The City, city state, or town: polis

Mark has "the whole city" in 1:33. In 1:45, Jesus could no longer enter a city/town. "The City" in 5:14 refers to the Decapolis (5.20) (*dekapolei*). At 6:33, people "ran to Jesus from all the towns/cities". 6:56 lists "where he went" as villages (*komas*), towns (*poleis*) or hamlets (*agrous*). At 14:13 and 14:16, "the city" is Jerusalem.

The town, market town: komopolis

In 1:38, Jesus says he must go on to "the next towns".

The village, unwalled neighbourhood: komé

In 6:6, Jesus "went about among the villages". At 6:36, the disciples suggest sending the 5,000 off to the hamlets (*agrous*) and villages to buy food. After 6:56 (see above), 8:23 has Bethsaida as the village out of which Jesus leads the blind man, forbidding him in 8:26 to return. In 8:27, Jesus and the disciples go to "the villages of Caesarea Philippi". At 11:2, two disciples in Bethphage and Bethany are sent to "the village opposite" to find the colt.

The place, neighbourhood, country: chora

At 1:5, "there went out from all the country of Judea ...". *Chora* is also the area of the Gerasenes (5:1) from which the demons beg not to be sent away (5:10).

Country farmstead, hamlet: agros

The word for field (*agros*) can mean "countryside", or "hamlet(s)", which is where the herdsmen flee (5:14), the place to which the disciples suggest the 5,000 are sent (6:36), the place from which Simon of Cyrene comes (15:21) – also in the list of 6:56.

Desert places: eremos

All these five terms refer to places of habitation, that is, places where various sizes of population are to be found. In Mark, these are contrasted with places without people, like the "desert place" or "wilderness" (*eremos*) where John the Baptist appears (1:3, 4) and Jesus goes (1:12, 13), or to which he escapes (*eremon topon*, 1:35; *eremoi topoi*, 1:45), or the "desert" (*eremon*) where the four thousand are (8:4).

From this survey, it is clear that so far as the ministry of Jesus is concerned, the Gospels have Jesus working in towns and cities, in villages, and in desert places. What is significant is that the Gospels never place Jesus in Sepphoris or Tiberias or Gaba, the great Roman cities. The only "city" to which Jesus goes is Jerusalem.

The actual locations for Jesus's ministry named in Mark are: on a hill (3:13; 9:2; 13:3), by the sea (often), in "the desert" (1:12; 1:35; 1:45; 6:31f; 8:4), "on the green grass" (6:39), or in villages and fields (1:38; 6:11; 6:36; 8:27; 11:1, 2, 11, 12; 14:3).

Generally, Mark's Jesus is negative about the city. The city is the place from which he withdraws (1:45; 6:33; 11:19; 13:1). He goes into it to condemn its temple (13:12), and uses an upper room there (14:13–15). Otherwise, Jesus lives at Bethany, outside Jerusalem, announces its destruction from "over against" it (13:3), gathers his disciples in a garden outside its walls (14:32), is taken from there under arrest (14:48–53), is condemned by its civil and religious authorities (14:53–15:20), and led outside it to be executed (15:21–41) and buried in a tomb on a hillside (15:42–47), where women disciples come to anoint his body (16:1–8).

Mark has a model of Jesus pressing into Gentile areas. In 7:24, Jesus leaves Capernaum (7:17) and goes to the region of Tyre, where he encounters the Syro-Phoenician woman (7:25–30), and then returns "by way of Sidon to the Sea of Galilee through the region of the Decapolis" (7:31), where he heals the deaf mute (7:32–37), feeds the four thousand (a number for Gentiles) (8:1–21), and cures the blind man near Bethsaida (8:22–26). Only in 8:10, 11–13 is Jesus briefly back in Galilee. Then, in 8:27–9:29, Jesus is in the villages of Caesarea Philippi (8:27), the territory of Herod Philip. When he eventually left that district and made a journey through Galilee, Jesus wished it to be kept secret (9:30). Again, at 10:1, he "left those parts and came into the regions of Judea and Transjordan". Already, Jesus had been "across the lake" (4:35), and in the area of the Gerasenes (5:1–20), both Gentile areas.

In Mark the later period in Gentile areas comes after the apparent ending to the successful Galilean ministry, which threatened to become oppressive (6:56), and equally after the persistent opposition of the Pharisees (7:1–25), and the dullness of the disciples (7:17–18). Again, after this "Gentile Mission" of 7:24–9:29, Jesus concentrates on individual contacts, followed by "going indoors" (9:33; 10:11), and then, from 10:32, by being "on the road", going up to Jerusalem (10:32).

Thus, Mark uses topography to indicate styles of mission.

> The geographical place names are coded descriptions of a mission which crosses boundaries – from Jewish territories west of Lake Galilee to Gentile territories to the north and east of the lake. (Geoffrey Harris: 137 in Vincent, 2006: 129–42).

Luke has a model of Jesus focusing on urban centres. At 4:43–44; Jesus says, "I must give the good news of the Kingdom of God to other towns (*polesin*) also, for that is what I was sent to do". So he gave the good news in the synagogues of Judea. At 10:1, 72 are approached to go in pairs to "every town (*polin*) and place (*topon*) he would himself visit". Indeed, the Mark 6:7–11 instructions to disciples as to how to act on being received into a house are in Luke 10:4–16 reformulated to apply to towns, as well as in 9:1–6 to houses. Again, Luke 13:22 has "Jesus went through the towns (*poleis*) and villages (*komas*) teaching, as he made his way to Jerusalem". This Lukan model of mission concentrating upon cities is continued in Acts. V. K. Robbins (in Alexander, 1991: 202–21) sees Luke–Acts as a "strategy of territoriality", a "narrative map", carrying out "the project inaugurated by Jesus of Nazareth" to "bring salvation and peace" to the eastern Roman Empire. Luke begins in Jerusalem (1:5–25) and ends there (24:50–51). Acts starts in Jerusalem (1:12–26) and ends in Rome (28:16–31). Luke uses the term "city" (*polis*) for Nazareth (1:26), Bethlehem (2:4, 11), Capernaum (4:31), Nain (7:11, 12), Bethsaida (9:10) and Arimathea (23:51). Twelve anonymous places are also called "city" (1:39; 4:43; 5:12; 7:37; 8:4, 27, 39; 10:1–12; 13:22; 18:1–3; 19:17–19).

Matthew also takes the story into the cities. Joseph and family move to "a city called Nazareth" (2:23). Jesus moves to Capernaum ("his own city") to commence his ministry (4:12–16) and later comes into "his own city" (9:1). Jesus is associated primarily with urban areas. He spends time at the lake (4:18–22; 8:18–27; 14:13, 22–28; 15:29–39), in remote areas (14:13–21), and in the hills (3:13; 14:22), but almost all of these stories have been taken over from Mark. Mark's "Jesus went around all the villages" is expanded to "*the cities* and villages" (9:35). The disciples are sent out on a mission to cities and villages (10:11), but all of the sayings refer to cities rather than villages (10:5, 14, 15, 23; 11:1, 20). Jerusalem is described as "the *holy* city" (4:5) and when Jesus enters it, "all the city went wild with excitement" (21:10).

Jesus and home

Capernaum (*kephar-nahum*, village of Nahum) was an important city in Galilee. On the north west of the Sea of Galilee, it was a major fishing port, as well as a commercial and regional centre. The plain of Gennesaret produces olives, dates and citrus fruit, while the northern hills provided black basalt stone for the buildings. Trade caravans from Egypt to Syria passed through the city. Travellers from the eastern territory of Herod Philip came to Capernaum as entry and customs station for the Roman province of Herod Antipas – cf. the call of Levi (2:13–17). There was a Roman garrison (cf. Lk. 7:2).

The town was established in the first century BCE. Remains of first century houses indicate black basalt stone buildings and paved floors, with roofs of wooden beams and straw thatch – easily removed (2:10). Several rooms, often four, were located around an open central courtyard, where fish hooks have been found. The complex would be workplace as well as residence for a dozen or more people, only some of whom would be a single "nuclear" family, others being probably relatives and co-workers. Archaeology shows a reconstruction of a first century "St Peter's House" at Capernaum. Its courtyard complex might have formed part of a larger "*insula*" group of complexes.

Jesus's background in building may well have given him images for his teaching. Parable-like references occur to building bigger barns (Lk. 12:18), constructing new towers (Lk. 13:4), finding foundations for new homes (Mt. 7:26), considering costs before embarking on building projects (Lk. 14:28), and viewing a city set on a hill (Mt. 5:14). All of these images also suggest that Jesus lived in an environment in which expansion and entrepreneurial building developments were a common occurrence.

In Mark, Jesus moves from his home town of "Nazareth in Galilee" (1:9). Although he remains "Jesus of Nazareth" (1:24; 10:47; 16:6), he moves to Capernaum (1:21), and makes his own home there (2:1). There, he taught and healed in the synagogue (1:21), did miracles (1:29–34), and much more (9:33–50). The remains of a synagogue in Capernaum date from the second or third century, but this basilica-type building may be on the site of an earlier one, which Jesus might have known. From the Gospels, it

cannot be stated with certainty whether the house at 2:1 was the property
of Jesus, or how long he used it as his "home". But Capernaum contained
also the house of Simon and Andrew (1:29), and possibly also James and
John. A kind of "community houses" pattern might well have developed in
Capernaum.

In Mark, the house is significantly the location for decisive parts of
Jesus's ministry. He ministers to the crowd there (1:32; 3:20), he banquets
with the excluded there (2:15; 14:3), he gives teaching to individuals there
(7:17; 9:33; 10:10). In each case, some house owner must have co-operated
so that the ministry could take place; or it took place in a home where one
or more disciples lodged with Jesus.

The house can also be a sign of unwillingness to share. The rich young
ruler possesses many *ktema* – estates, properties, lands (10:22). The temple
was meant to be "a house of prayer" (11:17), but now it is to be torn down
(13:2). The vanity of "building houses and planting vineyards" (Eccl. 2:4) is
radicalized now in the practice of the Son of Man:

> Foxes have holes,
> Birds of the air have nests,
> But the Son of Man has nowhere to lay his head. (Lk. 9:58)

For the disciple community, "leaving home" becomes a mark of obedient
and wholehearted following – a self-deprivation met by reception into the
"hundred" houses of the mini-Christian community.

> There is no one who has left house (*oikian*) or brothers or sisters or mother
> or father or children or lands (*agrous*), for my sake and the gospel's, who will
> not get back a hundred of such. Now, in this time – houses, brothers, sisters,
> mothers, children, lands – plus persecutions. (10:29–30)

Jesus had already announced in 3:35 "personal relationships richer a
hundredfold than those renounced", and claimed that "life" is already gifted
to them (9:43, 45), as they "receive the Kingdom of God" (10:15), which
Vincent Taylor says means "a richer social and religious fellowship", but not
"eternal life in the world to come" (Taylor, 1952: 434–35).

Mark insists that all these reversals and compensations happen now, "in
this time" (10:30). A new "home" was thus created, consisting of, perhaps,
a house he owned, the house of Simon and Andrew, and possibly other
homes nearby. Disciples had left their own homes and livelihoods, at least
for a time, and now had to depend upon alternative support. They
constituted his new family, as Jesus's "brother, and sister, and mother" (Mk
3:34–35), but they now were between themselves also a new family, with
houses, brothers, sisters and mothers, but significantly without wives or

fathers – missing from the list of 10:30. In an interesting study, Halvor Moxnes comments:

> The relations of authority and procreation are not included. These were the relations that were most closely associated with the normative structure of the household. The kingdom was not a mirror image of the patriarchal household, it transgressed its boundaries, it had a different composition, and it lacked its hierarchy. Therefore we may say that the household in the kingdom has been "queered". The traditional order has been questioned and twisted. (Moxnes, 2003:105; cf. Crossan and Reed, 2001: 94–96)

Jesus and disciples, by forsaking wives, have effectively "made themselves eunuchs" (Mt. 19:12). By having women in their company who "minister with them" (Mk 15:40–41) they clearly set up an alternative home, an alternative household. Shamed in his own home town (Mk 6:1–6), Jesus dislocates both men and women into a situation of liminality and marginality, where aspects of community life and 'having things in common' (cf. Acts 2:44) become part of the Kingdom experience. Denied honour in their own home town, family and home (Mk 6:4), the Kingdom servants create a new mini-society.

Luke develops this picture. Would-be disciples make excuses for not following on the grounds of commitments (Lk. 9:57; cf. Lk. 14:25–35). Families get divided (12:51–53), and "hating" them is necessary (14:26). Indeed, the "blessings" of being hated (6:22) are those of the disciple, those addressed in the "Beatitutes" (6:20), "blessings" which include poverty (6:20), hunger and anguish (6:21) (Moxnes, 2003: 62–63).

Jesus's home, and his disciples' homes doubtless, were not in the centre of power, but on the periphery. "Location, location, location" determines a great deal in the Jesus community reflected in the Gospels. In the 1970s we developed the saying at our inner city "alternative theological seminary", the Urban Theology Unit: "Where You Are Is Who You Are". Place is not just the passive background – it also determines to a considerable extent what happens and what people experience. Once the location is clear, what is going on is made clear. As Jesus says in Luke 7:28: "People who have fine clothes and live in luxury have their homes in royal palaces". If you have your home among the people, or among the poor, you act accordingly. And you then use the Gospel to answer the issues of the local people, or the poor, or the rich, depending on your location.

After location comes practice. Thus with the children in the marketplace in Luke 7:31–35, the decisive difference between the two groups of children is the action they are performing, the game they are playing. The kids playing the flute, so that people will dance, are the imitators of Jesus (the

Lord of the Dance!). The kids wailing, so that people will mourn, are the imitators of John Baptist (no bread, no wine!). Luke tends to support both lifestyles, as we shall see.

Jesus and Urban People

Galilee had six 'classes' of people: and all of them appear in Mark's story:
1. Rulers: Pilate, Herod Antipas, High Priests, Sanhedrin.
2. Retainers: Herodians, big landowners, merchants, tax officials.
3. Peasant farmers: small landowners.
4. Artisans: builders, craftsmen, often displaced farmers. (Pharisees often came from this 'class')
5. Labourers: displaced peasant farmers, jobless, day hired workers.
6. Excluded: lepers, ritually unclean workers, beggars, outlaws.

This can be seen in Stegemann and Stegemann (1999: 72, 135, 185). In reality, these groups can be reduced to three – 1. Rulers; 2. Retainers; and 3. Peasants (3, 4, 5 and 6).

Rulers

The rulers were the Romans and their co-operating elites who ruled from Jerusalem. Nearer to Galilee, Tiberias and Sepphoris were basically Roman cities with Herodian bureaucracies, through which technical, economic and cultural change was supported and administered, and from which the surrounding towns and villages derived a totally new orientation. The demands of the two cities changed the economic, agricultural and supply relationships and systems (McLennan, 1991). Traditional local Jewish peasants and Galileans hated both cities, not least because both were built and administered by alien Herodian/Idumean aristocracies, and both were supported by previously peasant retainers, such as stewards, tax collectors, toll officials, bodyguards and clerks, as much regarded as quislings by local patriots as treated as underlings by the largely imported ruling class. Rulers appear in Mark only as enemies or murderers, as with John the Baptist (6:14–29), Judas (14:10–11) and Jesus (14:53–15.20).

Retainers

Characters in the Gospel stories obviously belong to this retainer class who become tragic-comic heroes in the story. The agribusiness owner (5:11–13) and the merchants and money-changers (11:15–18) lose their business. William Herzog has developed detailed interpretations which show Jesus the parabler as "pedagogue of the oppressed", exposing current injustices.

The parable of the labourers in the vineyard (Mt. 20:1–15) exposes attitudes that blame the victim and keep day labourers separated and paralysed by self-hatred. The parable of the wicked tenants (Mk 12:1–12 and parallels) is about the spiral of violence and possibly peasant revolt. The parable of the rich man and Lazarus (Lk. 16:19–31) dramatizes the chasm that separates rich and poor and condemns the ideological justifications of that chasm. The parable of the unmerciful servant (Mt. 18:23–35) describes the mutual exploitation to which retainers are reduced, and critiques popular messianic expectations. The parable of the talents (Mt. 25:14–30, Lk. 19:11–27) praises the nevertheless futile effort of a whistle-blower to change business as usual (Herzog, 1994: 77–168).

Each of these parables indicates a Jesus taking sides with the exploited, and pointing up the injustices and victimizations which this world produces. They each dramatize the tragedy and futility of human attempts to deal with these situations, and negatively prepare the way for the radical reversals which are alone compatible with God's reign on earth, and indeed which become parts of it.

Beyond these exposures of systems of urban oppression, Jesus also describes the alternative, counter-hegemonic happenings of God's Kingdom, the new socio-political order. The parable of the Pharisee and the Publican (Lk. 18:9–14) shows an outcast successfully bypassing the Temple system of sacrifice and prayer, and obtaining God's acceptance; the persistent friend at midnight (Lk. 11:5–8) performs "limit acts that challenge the efforts of oppressors to dehumanise them", which "foreshadow a different order of human relations, moulded by justice and mutual reciprocity"; the unjust judge (Lk. 18:1–8) shows how shameless behaviour can succeed – "the widow has managed to break the mould"; the dishonest steward (Lk. 16:1–9) shows how "the weapons of the weak can produce results in a world dominated by the strong" (Herzog, 1994: 150–68, 214, 232, 258).

Peasants
Compared with Rulers and Retainers, the other groups were poor, and only got out of poverty by joining group 2, if they could.

There is a long tradition of the piety of the poor especially in the Psalms. *'Ebyon*, poor, occurs 28 times; *'ani*, wretched, occurs 38 times. These psalms were probably "pure liturgies of the word which will have taken place in the homes or meeting places of the religious groups from the lower class" (Albertz, 1994: 521–22). Certainly, the "occasional polemic against sacrifices (Pss 40:7–9; 69:31) could indicate that it did not take place in the Jerusalem temple". These "pious poor", or groups of *ch'sidhim* felt that God was particularly close to them (Pss 35:10; 140:13), and that he would deliver them (Ps. 10:4), so that they were "the real people of God" (Ps. 14:4). The peasant society and the poor in Jesus's day represented "a kind of shadow society" which "affords peasants an opportunity to profane the great tradition and subvert its power over their lives" by creating a powerful alternative but normative sub-culture (Herzog, 2004: 194).

Thus a new "place" is created, in opposition to Romans, temple and pharisaic synagogue. Several marks may be named:

1. Table fellowship, which in Pharisaic teaching meant keeping the temple's ritual purity laws in every household, is subverted by the meals with publicans and sinners, as the Pharisees themselves observe in 2:16. People excluded by the Torah are now included. Eating with tax collectors and people outside the law ("sinners") means creating a new table fellowship of Jesus: disciples and people from the lower groups of society.

2. The 12 tribal heads, a feature of the hoped-for restored Israel, are now seen in Jesus's 12, appointed "to be with him" (3:14). These men are obviously drawn from the lower classes of society, and represent an attempt to "cock a snook" against "top people" as the expected putative tribal heads of any reformed Israel (Vincent, 2008: 582–88). The new 12 tribes are led by people from groups 4, 5 and 6, and naturally may be expected to consist mainly of such people.

3. The Jesus movement (in Mk 3:17; 5:42; 7:11, 34; 14:36; 15:22, 36) uses Aramaic, alongside some Hebrew and a smattering of Greek, whereas the Pharisees and the Temple would have mainly used Hebrew. Again, Jesus's company would have used oral scripture traditions, while the Pharisees would also have used written texts. Moreover, the villagers' lives did not relate greatly to the cities. Thus, Jesus's work avoided the cities, and did not need the cities, as we have seen.

4. Money is not important, or is a tool in oppressors' hands. Missionaries do not need either money-bag (*pera*) or copper coins (*xalkon*). The widow's two *lepta* are the smallest coins (12:42). Wealth or possessions, *ktemata*, is what keeps the good man from following (10:17–22). Latin, the Roman language, is used in expressions at 12:42 and 15:16, and in words at 3:21; 5:9, 15; 6:27, 37; 7:4; 12:14; 15:15, 39, 44, 45. But all these are military terms – legion, soldier, flog, governor's palace, centurion, or commercial terms – measures, denarius, penny, tax. All relate to Roman military and commercial domination of the local population, especially its poorer members.

5. Images and parables come from peasant life. The sower in 4:1–19 has to sow on the rocky slope, as he has no flat, stone-free field to sow in. The seed growing secretly in 4:26–29 is perhaps a solitary result of such sowing in unwelcoming soil. The mustard seed is a weed, but welcome in inhospitable land as at least bringing some harvest. Peasants know about patching old clothes (2:21), pouring wine into wineskins (2:22), plucking corn (2:23), lighting a tiny lamp (4:21), measuring out grain (4:24), bleaching cloth (9:3) and millstones (9:42).

6. The Jesus movement appears to be continuing and championing the "little tradition" of peasant Galilee, which itself saw its origin in basic Israelite traditions such as Sabbath and Decalogue, but which distanced itself from the control of the Temple and the regulations of Pharisaism. The heroes of this basic Israelite tradition are claimed as Jesus's precursors.

> Jesus is implicitly and explicitly compared with Moses and Elijah, he declares the renewal of Israel underway (Lk./Q 13:28–29, 22:28–30), he presupposes and restates Mosaic covenantal teaching (Lk. 6:20–49; cf. Mt. 5), and (apparently) stands opposed to specifically Jerusalem institutions such as the Temple and high priests on the basis of an alternative understanding of Israel. (Horsley, 1995: 252)

Luke and Matthew

These attitudes which Mark attributes to Jesus are frequently continued in Luke, who has the Magnificat's "hungry filled with good things" (1:53), the "blessed are you poor" (6:20), and a constant plea to minister to the poor (6:27–36, 12:16–21, 14:7–14, 16:19–31), in whom blessedness resides. Luke has further subtleties, however, as we shall see (pp. 74–75, 78–79).

Matthew, however, is impressed by wealthy people. His parables are about rich people – a wealthy pearl merchant (13:45), farmers employing day labourers (13:24–30, 36–43; 20:1–16), graziers with flocks of one hundred sheep (18:12–14), wealthy absentee landlords (25:14–31) and wealthy rulers (18:23–35; 22:1–14; 25:31–36). This is very different from Mark's peasant economy.

Again, Matthew often speaks of money – "silver" eight times, "gold" and "talents". Whenever there are parallels to amounts of money in the Gospels, Matthew's are always the largest, with "talents" (Mt. 25:14–30) worth about fifty times more than Luke's "pounds" (Lk. 19:12–27). The wealthy ruler in the parable of forgiveness (18:23–35) forgives a debt of £20 million at today's rates! In the sending out of the disciples on mission, Mark says that they should take no copper money (Mk 6:8), Luke no silver money (Lk. 9:3), and Matthew no gold, silver or copper money (Mt. 10:9).

Matthew's Sermon on the Mount twice advises what to do in a lawsuit (5:25–26, 40) and the command is made to "give to anyone who asks" (5:42). Almsgiving is encouraged (6:2–4) and the Lord's Prayer focuses on a need to forgive our debtors (6:12). Mark's poor widow does not appear in Matthew. He has his own model disciple – Joseph of Arimathea, a "rich man" (27:57–61). The tax collectors and sinners who get to be with Jesus in the Kingdom (9:9–13), one suspects, might be Matthew's "poor in spirit" (5:3) rather than those who have actually become poor.

Jesus and Women

It is difficult to be sure as to whether attitudes to women among Jesus's Jewish contemporaries were radically different from those of the Greco-Roman world, where certainly the inferiority of women is assumed. Women of suitable status were married in their early teens – 12 to 16 was common.

Plutarch advises a man to "govern a wife, and at the same time delight and gratify her" (*Advice to Bride and Groom*, 35). Juvenal, however, writes his *Sixth Satires* bitterly complaining of women – "Their sins of lust are the least of all their sins" (*Satires*, 6.135). Demosthenes says, "men have wives to have children and be faithful guardians of the home, mistresses (*hetairai*) for pleasure, and concubines for the daily care of our bodies" (*Against Neaera*, 122). Women slaves were servants and/or concubines (Pomeroy, 1995: 150–63).

For the Jews, Josephus declares:

> The Law recognises no sexual connexions, apart from the natural union of man and wife, for the procreation of children. … The woman, says the Law, is in all things inferior to the man. (*Against Apion*, 2.199–200)

For adultery, Josephus goes on, "the penalty of death is inexorable". Josephus himself divorced a wife, "being displeased at her behaviour" (*Life*, 426). According to Mark 10:2–12, Jesus opposed divorce, as it contradicted the "one flesh" purpose of Genesis 1:27 and 2:24. This reflects the Roman situation which allows women to divorce their husbands, whereas Matthew 5:31–32 represents the Jewish Law which did not allow this.

In the limited one-roomed apartment or home, the wife's total life was taken up with husband, children, and usually assisting in the husband's work. In the larger house or villa, the wife was manager of the household, finance, and staff of slaves.

> Although in Rabbinic Judaism women are categorised with children and slaves for legal religious purposes, the biblical stories about women indicate that women were not perceived as minors or slaves in everyday life. (Schüssler Fiorenza, 1983: 109)

Schüssler Fiorenza quotes Ruth, Esther, Hannah, the mother of the seven sons in 2 Maccabees, and especially Judith, as heroic women leaders.

Women clearly play a major role in the Markan story of Jesus and his disciples. At the crucifixion, Mark records:

> A number of women were there, watching at a distance, among them Mary of Magdala, Mary the mother of James the younger and Joseph, and Salome, who had all followed him and served him in Galilee, together with several other women who came with him up to Jerusalem. (15:41)

The words for "followed" and "served" are highly charged in Mark. To follow – *akolouthein* – is the heart of discipleship, as in 1:18, and implies cross-bearing (8:34, 10:28), as well as belonging to Jesus's new family of relatives (3:20–35). To serve – *diakoneo* – is in Mark the task of angels (1:13), of Jesus himself (10:45), of the Twelve (9:35, 10:43), and of women like Simon's mother-in-law (1:31). To serve is to join with Jesus in his whole ministry (10:42). To "come with him" – *sunanabainein* – also implies a company of people, the word reappearing in Acts 13:31. Beside this group, it is a woman who anoints Jesus (14:3–9) and another who exposes Peter (14:53–54; 66–72). Two women witness his burial (15:47), and three women hear of his resurrection (16:1–8).

Mark has several important stories of Jesus and women – the healing of Simon's mother-in-law (1:29–31), the healing of the woman with the flow of blood (5:25–34), the raising of Jairus's daughter (5:21–24, 35–43), the Syro-Phoenician woman and her daughter (7:24–30), the poor widow (12:41–44), the woman who anoints Jesus (14:3–9). Each of the women illustrates discipleship at the margins, challenging those who seek status, guard the tradition, exclude outsiders, honour riches, or reject incomers (Mary Coates in Vincent, 2006: 79–97, 85–89). Each woman exhibits crucial elements of discipleship, acts suddenly, risks everything, precipitates herself unreservedly, "in faith". Indeed, three stories are of "women leading men" (Spencer, 2004: 47–75).

Susan Miller observes that the characteristics of persistence and determination are actually repeated in Herodias and her daughter (6:14–29), but their action "offers an evil counterpart to the faithful women we see elsewhere in the Gospel" (Miller, 2004: 198–99; Joynes in Vincent, 2006: 143–53).

Each woman allows Jesus to bring about New Creation, casting out evil, overcoming disease, and breaking barriers, overcoming prejudices, and allowing the last to be first (10:31).

> In Mark's Gospel women are excluded from positions of authority, but this situation enables them to develop relationships based on mutuality and reciprocity, ... and illustrate the self-giving which characterises the new creation. (Miller, 2004: 200)

The Alternative City

The expectation of Jesus is that there can be a new, more satisfactory, more just, situation in the human city. The image of the earthly Kingdom of God is indeed of a new and better human situation which affects everything, all places and all people. The Kingdom of God on earth, which Jesus embodies and proclaims, is initially God's gift of a prophetic and salvation-bringing project and community. When we pray "Your Kingdom come", it means the same as "Your will be done", which means moments, situations, communities, activities, projects and political actions in which for a short time the divine dynamic and blessedness take shape in a human, earthly context. The Kingdom comes whenever demons are cast out (Lk. 11:20). The Kingdom comes "in the midst of you" (Lk. 17:21).

This becomes clear in the beatitudes. For a start, Luke has Jesus saying the beatitudes "looking at the disciples" (Lk. 6:20). It is to them that he speaks when he says "Blessed are you poor, for the Kingdom of God belongs to you". And the disciples are poor because Jesus has just persuaded them to "give up all and follow me". The disciples now realize that each of the beatitudes indicates that people and communities which are regarded as being the excluded, in fact discover that they are precisely and exclusively those who are now the privileged in the new Divine Realm on earth, God's new Kingdom. Disciples who are hungry get food, those weeping get to laugh, those outlawed and hated get to dance for joy (Lk. 6:21–23). Whether these things apply to *all* poor people is not at all implied. However, what is certainly stated is that people doing well out of life will lose it all – the rich, the well-fed, those pleased with life, those spoken well of (6:24–26).

Discipleship has to participate in this Kingdom characteristic of reversals. People, places and occasions of apparent importance and significance are not so in the view of the Kingdom. Rather, a leper (1:40–45), a cripple (2:1–12), the unclean woman (5:25–34), the blind beggar (10:46–52), the poor widow (12:41–44) and a returning day labourer (15:21) encounter Jesus, and the poor, looking for a leader, get fed – 5,000 (6:30–44) and 4,000 (8:1–10).

Richard Horsley sees this "alternative city" of God's Kingdom as being fundamentally based on a return to essential and simple basics of Israel's original covenantal community.

> Jesus launched a mission not only to heal the debilitating effects of Roman military violence and economic exploitation, but also to revitalize and rebuild the people's cultural spirit and communal vitality. In healing various forms of social paralysis, he also released life forces previously turned inward in self-blame. In these manifestations of God's action for the people, and in his offering the kingdom of God to the poor, hungry, and despairing people, Jesus instilled hope in a seemingly hopeless situation. The key to the emergence of a movement from Jesus' mission, however, was his renewal of covenantal community, calling the people to common cooperative action to arrest the disintegration of their communities and to revitalize their cooperation and mutual support. (Horsley, 2003: 126-127).

This general picture is reflected in other writers (Herzog, 2000: 191–216; Freyne, 2004: 122–49; Sawicki, 2000: 134–98; Moxnes, 2003: 142–57).

Thus, the people, places and occasions significant for the Kingdom are those where the apparent powers are overthrown, and the otherwise insignificant, victimized, and unfulfilled people, places and occasions are raised up. These may be merely some oppressed group securing some justice for themselves. Or they may be some people acting significantly and salvifically among them. Or they may be people setting up projects of God's will, outposts of God's Kingdom, which will be embodiments of the Kingdom as counter-culture.

In every way, the alternative city of Jesus's Divine Realm reverses the politics and values of the city of his time. The political system of Judaism is based upon a divine legal code, administered by its accredited and often hereditary heads. For this, Jesus substitutes a political state determined by human love and by the imitation of a divine "Father". Jesus's kingdom is thus a force of radical humanization and secularization. The political system of Rome is based upon dominance, paternalism and the power of force. Jesus's alternative city is determined by each being the servant of the other and by lordship existing in servanthood, based on radical egalitarianism and "levelling". The social and economic systems of both Judaism and Rome are based upon the possession of land, wealth and appointment. Jesus substitutes a realm in which the poor and the "little ones" are privileged. Radical reversals are thus facilitated. Finally, the political power of established elites is ended. Judaism, Zealotism, Priesthood, Roman

authority all exist by honour and lordship within carefully demarcated
ethnic or power groups, for which Jesus substitutes those outside such
groups, the outsiders.

Thus, Jesus is a subversive within the city:

> He subverts the politics of Jewish authority by setting up his own free society
> of equals. He subverts the politics of Rome by setting up mutual servanthood
> in a new society. He subverts the politics of personal power, wealth and
> possessions by making the small and poor the centre of the Kingdom. He
> subverts the politics of elites by opening the Kingdom to those on the frontiers.
>
> And Jesus is also a community builder: The beginnings of a new system,
> the community of the disciples, disciples to the Kingdom, are set in motion.
> Everything that is needed for human life – society, politics, religion, sacredness,
> relationships – is now in the nascent community around himself. (Vincent,
> 2004: 79)

Thus Jesus, by his practice, sets up the alternative City. It is not primarily a
new religious entity, but a new community. But it is also a new reality
affecting everything by its alternative practice. "In the beginning is the
deed" (Stegemann and Stegemann, 1999: 204).

Jerusalem

Jerusalem in the time of Jesus bore the scars of many alien cultures, resulting
from its chequered history. After the exile in Babylon in 586 BCE, Jerusalem
was rebuilt under Persian rule from 538 to 333 BCE. Alexander the Great
then established Hellenistic rule from 333 to 63 BCE, but Jerusalem itself
was redeveloped under the Maccabeans from 175 to 63 BCE. The Roman
Emperor Pompey conquered the country in 63 BCE, and the land remained
under Roman rule until 334 CE, despite the Jewish revolt of 66–70 CE,
which ended in another destruction of Jerusalem.

The Jewish Roman vassal King Herod the Great, 40–6 BCE, strengthened
Jerusalem and built a huge palace for himself, the Caesarium and the
Agrippium, named after his Roman benefactors. This was the palace of
Pilate, the Procurator in Jesus's time. Herod also built the massive temple
on Temple Mount, with a huge Roman fortress, the Antonia, north of it,
"the barracks" of Acts 21:37.

Jerusalem (*Ierousoluma*), according to Mark, is among the list of places
from which "great crowds heard what he was doing and came to see him"
(3:8). Scribes came down from Jerusalem to question him (3:22 and 7:1).
Later, Jesus and the disciples are "going up to Jerusalem" (10:32, 33; 11:1)
and then "came into Jerusalem" (11:15, 11:27). Women "came up with him

to Jerusalem" (15:41). Jerusalem is the place where the alternative community being set up by Jesus comes into most clear opposition to the great city. The alternative Messiah is heralded by his followers as a new David (11:1–10). The old order in the temple is symbolically displaced (11:15–18). Religion's control over the afterlife is repudiated (12:18–27). The Davidic supremacy is ended (12:35–37). The stewardship of the rich is exposed (12:41–44). The temple is replaced (13:1–2). Meantime, Jesus has his own private anointing outside the temple (14:3–9), arranges an alternative Passover (14:12–16) and institutes his substitute Passover (14:17–25). Jesus has "bypassed the cult" (Dunn, 2003: 786–88).

Jesus thus, in Jerusalem itself, draws up the lines of his alternative society and communion. He sets out his own stall – the ass, the cleansing, the anointing, the last supper. He exposes the existing powers – the temple, the Romans, the chief priests, the Pharisees, Herodians, Sadducees and scribes. He sets up alternative objects as models – the child, the colt, the little ones, the anointing woman, the widow. He sets up a place where these alternative political realities can be acted out and supported – the disciple group (Vincent, 2004: 77–79).

Thus, for Jesus, God's Alternative City (pp. 68–70) replaces Jerusalem. Yet in his own lifetime, it was the city of God, and the centre of power religious and secular, where High Priests, elders, lawyers – "the whole Council" – condemn him (14:53–15:1), and secure a death sentence from Pilate (15:2–20).

After 70 CE Jerusalem remained in ruins, and the Romans set up a meeting of Pharisees at Jamnia to organize a non-temple Judaism. A Roman attempt to build a temple of Jupiter on the Temple Mount led to the Bar-Kochba revolt in 130 CE, after which Judeans were banned from Jerusalem, and Jupiter's temple was completed – as Jesus is reported as predicting in Mark 13:14. Jerusalem became a totally non-Jewish city, with a temple to Aphrodite on the traditional site of Golgotha (Harding, 2001: 93–97; Crossan and Reed, 2001: 182–229).

A consequence of Jerusalem's constantly threatened and violated role as holy city was that it came to play a decisive role in apocalyptic literature, which flourished from the third century BCE at least until 120 CE. Apocalyptic cosmic transformations of Israel often include a renewed Jerusalem, in the midst of many Persian and Hellenistic elements. The apocalyptic Jerusalem is raised to the highest mountains in Zechariah 14:16–19 and Isaiah 40:4, and achieves its paradisal form in Ezekiel 47. This ideal city attracts the nations in Isaiah 56:1–8, a picture repeated in Revelation 21–22.

However, as with 2 Esdras 9:38–10:45, the "new Jerusalem coming down out of heaven from God" of Revelation 21:2 and 10, is not an actual earthly city. The city is the "Bride of the Lamb" (21:9) and thus is merely another symbol of the eschatological union of the faithful with the Lord. The walls of jasper, city of gold, foundations of jewels of Revelation 21:18 are clearly not an actual city of Jerusalem, but an ideal location beyond history, designed for those written in the Lamb's book of life (21:27). The city is one of several images of "God dwelling with people, face to face", as in 21:3–4. The image of the heavenly city in Revelation is thus, like other images in apocalyptic literature, a way of envisioning a future spiritual situation which will compensate for the hopelessness of the earthly Jerusalem, ravaged and left desolate by the Roman armies. The picture does not add to our material concerning the city, therefore, but belongs with all other images in Revelation to some imaginary but promised transformed reality, to compensate for the desolation being experienced in the real city.

Which Gospel?

To "make connections" we need to do a Situation Analysis of our own context, and also a Situation Analysis of a biblical piece (see below, pp. 102–07). What guidance can we derive from what we know of each of the Gospels, to discover which of them might be the most useful, constructive and challenging dialogue partner for ourselves in our contemporary context?

To do this, we are not necessarily dependent upon any view of the sort of community for which a particular Gospel was written (Bauckham, 1998: 9–48). Rather, I am suggesting that certain characteristics of the different Gospels might be taken into account by people today, when they are deciding which Gospel to take as their dialogue partner. Any conclusions regarding possible first century receiving communities might be highly questionable, but the diverse character of the Gospels themselves is not. Neither is their potential for dynamic engagement with contemporary disciples and practitioners.

Thus, regardless of how the different Gospel versions of the Jesus stories and Jesus tradition were received by the communities, behind or in front of the Gospel writers, we today can use them to reflect upon our own contextual experience. We may discern different styles of spirituality in each Gospel (Barton, 1992). or the varied versions of Christian discipleship there (Howard-Brook and Ringe, 2002; Segovia, 1985: 102) or the different strategies for mission described or implied (Harris, 2004). What has so far not been extensively worked at is the question of the practice and politics implicit in each Gospel (Rowland in Vincent, 2006: 3–8; Joynes in Vincent, 2006: 114–47). It is precisely this last element which is of interest to us, if we are seeking to imagine how the varied Gospel sagas actually worked out in terms of practical engagement for a disciple or disciple group in the community, social and political spheres. We have, therefore, few travelling partners so far to guide us. Hopefully, the Reception History of the Gospels will tell us elements of what Christians historically have done because of the Gospels, rather than just what their commentators have written about them (Vincent, 2005: 10–11, 33–35).

Mark

Conceivably written with the Roman and Hellenistic "Son of God" figure in mind, Mark's Gospel (c. 68 CE) features Jesus as a peasant small-town leader who, like Moses and Elijah, pioneers a renewal of the community of Israel among the peasant class. The story seeks to support and replicate such a community in Gentile Christian communities. There are two major elements: first, the confirmation and re-establishment of a divine covenantal community among the unprivileged; and, second, the calling of a smaller number of community servants, like the Twelve, who act as provokers, sustainers and leaders of the wider covenantal community. Thus, there are two sets of models, paradigms and exemplary happenings which the Christian communities are to use to regulate, confirm and act out their commitment to the Way (Horsley, 2001: 1–5).

Mark has been somewhat neglected through the centuries by those seeking to "make connections". It had sparse reading in churches – Matthew was the favourite for lectionaries, followed by Luke and John, leaving Mark's unelaborated and often undeveloped stories unheard. Only in the past century has Mark been heard as a solo – as it can be, because it alone has no dependence on the other Gospels or on any other known source. Inasmuch as most of our treatment has been of Mark's Gospel, we pass on to the others.

Matthew

Matthew (c. 85–95 CE) is written to show Christians that they are the true successors to and inheritors of the Old Testament. Ten times Matthew has "this took place to fulfil what the Lord had spoken by the prophet …". There are many other Old Testament allusions. The Gospeller "brings from his treasure new things and old" (13:52). Jesus has come, not to destroy the Law, but to "complete" it (5:17). So the Sermon on the Mount (5:1–7:37) continues and brings to fruition the Law given on Sinai (Exod. 24:7). Christians still observe the Sabbath (24:20), and practise alms-giving, prayer and fasting (6:1–18). But their claim to be still members of the Jewish community has become impossible after the Christians' exclusion from the synagogues in 85 CE. So Matthew argues that Christianity has now supplanted Judaism, and has a better righteousness (5:20).

Matthew thus addresses the needs of mainly urban Christian communities, probably of Gentiles as well as former Jews, to explain how they must conduct their lives. He relocates Mark's stories in urban situations, with urban characters, and even changes the currency. The Christians may be both settled congregations and wandering radical missionaries (Luz, 1994: 39–56; Theissen, 1978). Regarding possible concern with or relevance to the wider life of the urban communities in which they live, Matthew's advice is clear. Disciples are the light of the world, their works make people glorify their heavenly Father (5:14–16), and their fruits determine their final destiny (7:15–20), the law of love (7:21–23) issuing in care for others (25:31–46), even if these are likely to be only "my brothers" – that is, fellow Christians. Christians live in a world in which persecution and opposition from both secular and religious powers comes to followers, as they did to Jesus (10:16–25). They must react as he did, with love, even love of enemies (5:43–48).

Luke

Luke (c. 75–85 CE) features Jesus who began life in Jerusalem and the temple (especially Chapter 2), journeying towards it (9:51—19:48) and ministering in the temple (19:47–48; 21:37–38). After his death, the disciples do not leave for Galilee (as in Mark 14:28; 16:7), but remain in Jerusalem (24:50–51).

Luke puts Jesus into Jewish and human history (1:5; 2:1; 3:1–2), and the "history of salvation" embraces all humanity. It was not some insignificant happening (Acts 26:26), but one that people like Agrippa might believe (Acts 26:29). Jesus has become in Hellenistic terms the Great Benefactor, and disciples should follow. Luke tells rural stories adapted to urban living. In Mark 10:30, Peter the fisherman's "giving up all" became giving up lands, but in Luke 18:29, fields and lands have disappeared. Urban Gentile cities are now the scene.

Jesus in Luke is critical of Herod – "that fox" (13:32), and does not defer to Pilate (23:1–25). By emphasizing love over violence, generosity over riches, human need over Law, equality over class, new relationships rather than hierarchy, Jesus carries a strong critique of Rome:

> By espousing radically new social patterns and by refusing to defer to the
> existing political authorities, Jesus pointed the way to a social order in which
> neither the Romans nor any other oppressing group would be able to hold
> sway. (Cassidy, 1978: 79)

Luke's Jesus calls his communities to personal and community lifestyle
alternatives, but "little or nothing suggests that his programme of reform
involved a socio-political upheaval that could be regarded as a serious
threat to the stability of this region of the Roman empire", so that the
early Christians "took over very smoothly the morality which prevailed
in the Greco-Roman world and adapted it into their new vision" (Prior,
1995: 195).

John

John (c. 100 CE) develops the Synoptic Gospels' opposition between
Galileans and Jerusalem elites. Seventy times, John refers critically to "the
Judeans" – *Ioudaioi*, who Josephus says were the elite group which returned
from exile and built and then ran the temple (Ashton, 1991: 153).

Jesus criticizes his opponents for not following "your Law" (7:19; 8.17;
10:34), for their futile claim to be "children of Abraham" (8:33). Christian
believers who are Pharisees must renounce their Pharisaism (3:1–11; 9:40–
41; 12:42–43; 19:38–42). In fact, Christians are being expelled from the
Synagogue (*aposunagos*: 9:28; 12:42; 16:2) and even killed (16:2; cf. 10:30).
To be a Christian is a matter of "new birth" (1:11–13; 3:3–8: 9:2–7). To
remain with "the Judeans" is thus "not a matter purely of religion or
geography but of ideological choice" (Howard-Brook, 1994: 43).

The ideological choice of John and his community is "participation in
the formation of a new religion based on discipleship to Jesus". Because of
this, the community has been expelled from Judaism, and has abandoned
Judean feasts like Sabbath, Passover, Tabernacles and Dedication, and built
a new unity around its own rituals – baptism, eucharist, foot-washing and
its life as fulfilling that of its Master (18:9, 32) (Howard-Brook, 1994:
49–50). The community around whom John's Gospel was written has
been described thus:

> It was a community of both men and women, of Jew and Gentile and Samaritan.
> Some of the members certainly must have been deeply familiar with the
> biblical tradition. Given the absence of stories focusing on economic
> conditions, it was probably a relatively prosperous group, in contrast with
> the Markan or Lukan communities, which seem to have included many of
> the Palestinian poor. At the same time, Jesus expressly notes the long-term
> presence of the poor "with you" (12.8), a technical term indicating that the

poor were not simply present in the society but were a part of the Johannine community (cf. 9:40; 18:5, 18). Thus, in every way possible within the universe of its time, the gospel's primary social group was multicultural. (Howard-Brook, 1994: 49)

Fernando Segovia sees the Johannine Community as "a sectarian group with a predominantly introversionist orientation", which reflects that not everyone can undergo a change of heart, though they must continue to seek to gather "the sheep" out of "the world" (Segovia, 1985: 102). The world as such is of little concern, except as the environment for people "believing" (3:16). Jesus's claim to bring the Kingdom of God to this earth has been transformed and spiritualized. You "see" the kingdom of God if you are "born from above" (3:3); and it is not a worldly phenomenon at all (3:3–12). "My kingdom is not of this world", says the Johannine Jesus (18:36).

Making Connections

When we "make connections" with a text, we need to be sure that we have a realistic picture from a "Situation Analysis" of ourselves.

So, when looking at a text, we study "our reality". This might consist of a variety of elements, including gender and sexuality, ethnicity, age, ability, wellbeing, socio-economic status, political affiliation and denominational, spiritual and theological traditions (Holgate and Starr, 2006: 91–108). Beyond this we need to "read our situation" through social analysis, which includes questions about our social, economic, political and cultural contexts (Holgate and Starr, 2006: 109–14) – and then, the interpretations of those in contexts different from our own, especially in the global, post-colonial, and vernacular perspectives (Holgate and Starr, 2006: 115–32, 122–52).

In fact, this is exactly what happens in the city. Contemporary disciples "make connections" between Gospel contexts, missions and lifestyles, and their own, as a "Practice Reception History" of their uses indicates..

Mark

A recent example of "making connections" is the collection *Mark: Gospel of Action* (Vincent, 2006). I give two of the "community responses".

Christopher Burdon connects with Mark's communities (Burdon in Vincent, 2006: 176–87). He sees Mark's community as having many connections, not so much with large churches or institutions, but with "small learning groups, activist organisations, local parishes and alternative religious communities" (Burdon in Vincent, 2006: 178). In each of these, he sees Markan characteristics – a debate about leadership, "powerless power", the crossing of boundaries, and "provisionality in politics and liturgy". A small Christian community today could learn much from how these elements appear in Mark.

Ian Wallis sees his congregation at Houghton-le-Spring as very like the mix of all sorts and conditions of people in the Gospel, and then seeing how Mark "helps us to discover Jesus in our Galilees", (Wallis in Vincent, 2006: 188–97, 191) which means:

> Within the relatively safe environment of a church community and taking Mark's Gospel as our script, enabling Jesus to become visible as we attempt to act out our lives through faith as fully and wholeheartedly as he performed his. (Wallis in Vincent, 2006: 197)

These elements of community and faith practice mean that Mark's Gospel particularly finds a home in the discipleship, spirituality and mission practice of urban disciples. The work of many colleagues in the Urban Theology Unit may be cited, especially that of Laurie Green, Ian Duffield and Andrew Davey, beside the pioneering work of Ched Myers (Davey, 2001: 66–73; Duffield and Pagan, 2008; Green, 2003: 81–95; Myers 1988).

Mark's striking exposure of Roman power has recently found contemporary connections in the areas of American or Western imperialism, global capitalism and ecological concerns (Crossan, 2007: 209–17; Horsley, 2003: 137–49; Miller in Vincent, 2006: 154–63; Myers in Vincent, 2006: 164–75; Wilde 2006: 164–75).

Matthew

Matthew has been frequently "picked up" in religious community "Rules", by sectarian churches in writing their "Disciplines" and, at the other end of the spectrum, by churches which have become "national churches", in their "Laws Temporal and Spiritual" (Luz, 1994: 23–38). Matthew suits denominations or ecclesial bodies which see themselves as setting up a Christian city, or a Christian state, as in John Calvin or the Founding Fathers of the USA. But the nature of that Christian city based on Matthew will usually be marginal, unless backed up by a co-operating dictatorial secular power as, in principal at least, with national or state churches. A recent commentator concludes:

> Matthew's gospel is a counter-narrative. It is a work of resistance written from and for a minority community of disciples committed to Jesus, the agent of God's saving presence and empire. The gospel shapes their identity and lifestyle as an alternative community. (Carter, 2004: xvii, cf. 1, 3)

Matthew thus lends itself to use by strongly liturgical, disciplined churches, especially those that trust in or create a political situation in which they play or try to play a decisive role. Where this is not possible in the public realm, then Matthew serves equally strongly to determine the life and community patterns and structures of intentional or even strict confessional communitarian or sect-like communities.

Luke

Luke and Acts typically suit many conventional churches which have a good mix of people involved in Christian living at a variety of different levels in society. Luke is clear. Jesus has good news for the poor. And Jesus calls people to costly discipleship. The three failed disciples are only in Luke (9:57–62). And Luke's special emphases touch the poor, and women, and those needing healing.

But these pieces of Gospel are hidden in a narrative which is addressed to "most excellent Theophilus", and which has many elements of classic suburban living, with all its inevitable compromises. It is a Gospel *about* the poor rather than of the poor or for the poor. And its call to discipleship as "Take up your cross *daily*" (9.23) is a far cry from the once-for-all cross-taking of Mark.

Anthony Harvey muses over Luke's sayings, "Sell *everything* you have and distribute it to the poor" (18:22), and "Sell your possessions and give alms" (12:33), which might mean inviting the poor (14:13), as in the Great Supper (14:16–24).

> But at the same time it is Luke who makes it clearest that obedience to Jesus' teaching did not *always* imply such a radical response. It is Luke who gives us the saying, "Beware of all covetousness, for it is not from the *superfluity* of possessions that a man gains life" (12:15) – the clear implication being that we retain enough to live on, and give away the *surplus*: this was the mistake of the Rich Fool, who tried to hoard his surplus instead of distributing it as alms, and (probably) of the rich man in the parable, who could well have afforded to feed Lazarus out of his surplus without diminishing his capital. It is Luke also who interprets Jesus' saying, "Give to him who asks" in terms of offering loans in situations where there will be no advantage and perhaps little security: it is desirable and commendable to remain in the position of being *able* to make loans, which precludes dispersing one's capital through profligate almsgiving. In Luke, that is to say, we have the radically unrestricted maxim but also a repertory of moral injunctions aimed, not (as in Matthew) at those who are materially destitute or who have attempted to take the general maxim literally by distributing their capital assets, but at those who are in a position to give large suppers, to offer generous loans and to achieve a high standard of regular almsgiving. (Harvey, 1990: 126)

Harvey concludes: "Sell everything you have" is "a piece of typical moralist's hyperbole", and some sayings are for "the much smaller circle of those who abandoned their usual work and responsibilities in order to become Jesus' personal followers" (Harvey, 1990: 126).

To others, Luke inspires a mission of discovery through journeys. Be saved by a foreigner (to Jericho, Lk. 10:25–37), protest against powers (to Jerusalem, Lk. 19:23), be open to strangers (to Emmaus, Lk. 24:13–35), listen to black disciples (to Africa, Acts 8:26–30), be ready for conversion (to Damascus, Acts 9:1–9) (so Greg Smith in Vincent, 2003: 100–19, 110–15).

John

John has been dubbed "the spiritual gospel". Hence it has tended to be used by people who have vocation or leisure to meditate and create. It is the Gospel for people on retreat or into reflection in depth.

Wes Howard-Brook on John seeks to follow how "the Word becomes Text" and "the Word as Text becomes Flesh". Only John has "My kingdom is not of this world" (18:36). The Christians indeed form an "alternative community", but all the references are to the special benefits of the disciple community, who receive him (1:12), see his glory (1:14), receive from his fullness (1:16), and know his testimony is true (21:24). Disciples are to be "kept in the world", rather than be taken out of it (17:15). But while they must be *in* the world, they must be not *of* the world (3:16–21; 17:16–18). They must even love the world that persecutes them (20:21–23).

Out of this, it is hard to read a strong emphasis on practice, except as witness; or upon political involvement, except as forced by enemies. Yet John's Gospel has inspired compassionate mystics and practical gurus – and also communities of radical discipleship:

> John's Gospel stands as a powerful invitation to resist the seductiveness of all death-dealing cultures, including our own. In its place, it offers the intimacy of community life grounded in the love of God. (Howard-Brook, 1994: xvii)

Coherence with God's Project

Christian behaviour is based upon the disciples' conformity, in their own widely differing contexts, with the directions and concerns of Jesus as revealed in the Gospels as a kind of "continuation" or "outworkings" or "correspondence" (Luz, 1994: 82; Vincent, 2005: 3–8). Coherence with God's Project means for the Christian disciple coherence with Jesus's Project to embody, precipitate and provide a community for God's newly present

Kingdom. In practice, responsibility for the city means that the disciple always has to work towards this coherence on two levels.

First, the disciple acts on the level of the immediately presenting issue, and tackles both the needs of the person and also their relationships to the community. This is never a superficial or immediate "solution". It takes not only the individual person's need seriously, but also all the factors involved in that person's problem, failure or incompleteness.

On this level, the pattern of Jesus dealing with a person in his or her situation is important. In Mark, but also often in Luke and Matthew, a consistent pattern is described, with Jesus being described as performing a series of actions. Jesus thus (Vincent in Rowland and Vincent, 2001: 101–11, 106):

1. speaks to people by name;
2. deals with the presenting situation;
3. heals the sufferer;
4. calls the healed person to new life;
5. secures a new future for the victim;
6. asserts the new community of the healed;
7. challenges the powers that were victimizing; and
8. confronts the critics.

The individual Christian citizen/disciple seeks to "bring change" to people and situations of need, wherever they are, by following this Jesus model pattern of action. Each of the eight elements may not be possible each time. The Gospel stories do not always name all of them. But the Jesus follower gets in as much as she/he can, imitating in some way the practice of Jesus, following what Miroslav Volf describes as "As Christ acts ... So we act" (Volf, 1996). This is what the disciple tradition in the Gospels opens up (Howard-Brook and Ringe, 2002). The term "Imitation" of Jesus or Christ has usually meant a more spiritual and often passion-centred "following", although Richard Burridge has used the term "Imitation" for this kind of practice-oriented following (Burridge, 2007: 73–78).

However, there is always also a second level, where the citizen/disciple moves beyond a ministry to the needy individual or group in their situation, and seeks to bring change to the wider context of people and institutions in the city. The citizen/disciple therefore also:

1. names the real oppressors;
2. deals with the social and political situation;
3. heals all in a similar state;
4. calls communities to wholeness;
5. secures new futures for communities;

6. creates faith communities of the newly franchised;
7. tackles the wider economic controllers; and
8. debates with the critics and media.

Each singular scenario now becomes part of a wider "Project" – both negatively and positively. In Matthew, for instance, the disciple discerns the present city and state, as the false "centre" of society.

> The gospel's divine point of view exposes and evaluates this centre negatively as a world that dominates, oppresses, marginalises, destroys. It elevates male above female, king above people, ruler above ruled, rich above poor, religious leaders above people, violence above compassion, the centre above the margins. (Carter, 2004: 3)

All of this the gospel community "resists and subverts". Positively, Justice in Matthew denotes "God's will or saving reign enacted in human actions" in the midst of the city:

> Righteousness or justice (3:15; 5.6) means reconciling and faithful relationships (5:21–26, 27–32), integrity of one's word (5:33–37), non-violent resistance to evil (5:33–37), love and prayer for one's enemy (5:43–48), mercy in giving alms (6:2–4), prayer (6:5–15; 7.6–11), fasting (6:16–18), an anxiety-free existence trusting God (6:19–34), refraining from judging others (7:1–5). (Carter, 2004: 13)

Each Gospel in its different way invites participation in the practice of Jesus. At every point, the disciple is called to *discern* where and how the particular issue with which connection is made is indicative of the larger issue of the divine project on earth, visible in the practice and mission of Jesus.

Chapter 6

The City and the First Christians

A Mission to Cities

The events concerning Jesus and his Galilean followers became part of a much wider history and movement, precipitated by the stories of what happened after the fateful closing days of Jesus's life in Jerusalem, probably in the year 33 CE. We know of those events from two primary but very different sources.

First, we have the two-volume work of Luke. The first volume, Luke's Gospel, records "what Jesus did and taught" in Galilee (Acts 1:1), being "a prophet mighty in deed and word" (Lk. 24:19), continuing after his resurrection in Jerusalem (Lk. 24:1–53). The second volume, Acts, reassembles the followers (Acts 1:12–26), and tells their spirit-inspired story, first in Jerusalem, and then spreading out to the rest of Judea and beyond. Luke wrote his works around 75–85 CE.

The second witness is much earlier – notably Saul of Tarsus, a Pharisee who first persecuted Christians (Gal. 1:13–14) and then became one (Gal. 1:15–17). Parts of his story are told in Acts, but there are many discrepancies between the accounts in Acts and what is implied in Paul's letters. Paul's letters probably date from 45–55 CE.

The story of Acts is almost totally an urban story. The many languages of Acts 2:5–13 originate in 15 diverse cities and areas. Stephen's message in Acts 7:2–53 is that God has consistently preferred places and people outside Israel. Acts 8 brings in the excluded Samaritans (cf. Acts 1:8; Jn 4), and then the Ethiopian finance minister from the desert city of Gaza (8:26–40). Saul of Tarsus in Asia Minor is converted on his way to Damascus (Acts 9:1–9) and is sent to Arabia for three years – to learn his theology(?) (Gal. 1:17). Jerusalem the city is the base for the first "Council" (Acts 15:1–35). Caesar's "free city", the great multicultural city of Antioch, with its Greek, Syrian, Jewish, Latin and African suburbs (Richard Longenecker in Harrison, 1985) is the site of a significant multi-cultural ministry team:

> Now in the Church at Antioch there were prophets and teachers, notably:
> Barnabas (of Cyprus), Simeon the Black, Lucius from Cyrene, Manaen from
> Herod's court, and Saul (of Tarsus). (Acts 13:1)

Luke has a "Jerusalem focus", and he has Paul in Jerusalem more than we
would expect from the Epistles, with Paul, like Jesus, doing a "long-drawn-
out final journey to Jerusalem" (Acts 20:21; Alexander, 2006: 13, 229).

The earliest Christian groups were known as followers of "the Way"
(Acts 9:2, 19:9, 23; 24:14, 22; William Klassen in Hill 1998: 94–96; Stegemann
and Stegemann, 1999: 91–105), or adherents of the sect of the Nazarenes
(Acts 24:5, 14). At Antioch, a group of (probably gentile) disciples "were
first called Christians" (Acts 11:26, cf. 26:28). At Antioch, too, the ex-
Pharisee Paul worked (Acts 11:25–30, 13:1–3, 15:35) as an "apostle to the
gentiles" (Rom. 11:13), operating from a joint Jewish–Gentile Christian
community (Gal. 2:12–16).

Most of the followers seem to have lived in urban areas, where there
were Jewish communities also. Membership in the new community meant
table-fellowship in each other's homes, regardless of previous status (Gal.
2:11–14). Those who are "in Christ" and "in the Lord" are all the same (Gal.
3:27–28), "one body" (1 Cor. 10:17), the continuing earthly "body of Christ"
(1 Cor. 12:27), which might one day incorporate all humanity (Rom. 5:12–
21) as well as all Israel (Rom. 11:26). Indeed, Jews who do not join this new
body are no longer the descendants of Abraham (Gal. 3:6–4.6), inheritors
of God's promise (Gal. 3:29), or children of the true Jerusalem (Gal. 4:26).
Without having undergone the rite, Christian gentiles are "the
circumcision" (Phil. 3:3). They are a "covenanted people", "blood-brothers"
and "blood-sisters" (1 Cor. 11:25; Mk 14:22–24, etc.).

The Christians thus developed a "citizenship" in the same way as the
Jewish diaspora did – not on the basis of any official civic, geographical or
neighbourhood separateness, but by themselves setting up self-created
boundaries which separated them from those who lived around them, in
the same way as the Jews. For the Christians, the boundaries were
commitment to Jesus, baptism, belonging to a house church, participating
in ministry or "work" on the Word, the reading of gospel stories or epistles,
and sharing in the common meals.

> This new group identity "in Christ" provides a social identity that cuts across
> and encompasses previous social identity distinctions (Gal. 3:28). Yet at the
> same time it establishes a new boundary between insider and outsider, a
> boundary that in ideological terms owes much to its Jewish roots, built upon
> the contrast between the idolatry and depravity outside the group, and the

> holiness and righteousness within. (David Horrell in Blasi *et al.* 2002:
> 309–35, 332; cf. Meeks, 1983: 159–60).

Diaspora Jews had their own neighbourhoods, civil associations, and schools. They usually secured exemption from offering sacrifices to the emperor or to local gods (thus being called "atheists"). Many perhaps, like Paul, were Roman citizens. Before he died in 37, Tiberius had suppressed both Judaism and the Egyptian mystery cults for their "superstitious beliefs" (Suetonius, *Life of Tiberius*, 36). From 38 to 41 CE, civil disturbances involving Jews erupted in Alexandria, Antioch, Asia Minor and Rome itself. Gaius Caligula, emperor 37–41 CE, opposed any "gods" but himself, and was only with some difficulty persuaded by Philo not to put his own statue in the Temple at Jerusalem (*Legatio ad Gaium*, 157).

Sympathetic gentiles who did not fully convert (which necessitated circumcision) were known as "God-fearers", and it was to these that the Christian missionaries went first (Acts 10:2, 22, 35; 13:16, 26). Similar people are also called "devout" (from *sebomai*) at Acts 13:43, 50; 16:14; 17:4, 17; 18:7; 22:12 (Crossan, 2007: 154–58; Crossan and Reed, 2005: 23–26; Harding, 2003: 289–90).

Jews, God-fearers and Christians were suspect as not worshippers of the Roman emperor as God. Philo and some influential Alexandrian Jews met with Gaius to defend their rights. Gaius asks:

> Are you the god-haters, who do not know me as a god,
> a god acknowledged by all others, but not named by you?

The Jews reply that they offer sacrifice for the emperor. "But not *to* me", retorts Gaius (*Legatio ad Gaium*, 353, 357).

The Praetorian Guard assassinated Gaius and appointed Claudius, who ruled from 41–54. In a letter to Alexandria, the new emperor warns people not to upset the rights of Jews, who had lived there for many years, and were allowed to follow their traditional religious customs. However, he also prohibited any further Jewish immigration. According to Suetonius, Claudius also expelled Jews from Rome because of an ongoing disturbance caused by *Chrestus* (*Claudius*, 25). Arguably, this refers to Christians, and would be the first non-Christian reference to Christianity.

Nero (54–68), Claudius's son, was declared emperor at 17 years of age. Claudius was confirmed as a "god manifest" after his death, but Nero was happy to be "good spirit of the world and source of all good things", though soon also "son of god". In 64, he started (according to Dio Cassius 62.18.1) the nine-day fire that ravaged Rome and gave him space for his "new city", the Golden House, 125 acres of park and buildings for himself. Tacitus

(*Annales*, 15.44) says that to deflect the blame from himself, Nero accused people "known for their shameful deeds, whom people call Christians (*Christiani*)" Tacitus records Nero's punishment of the Christians – being covered with wild beast skins and torn to death by dogs, or being crucified and burned as human torches.

This kind of event seems not to have been repeated at any time in the first century. Pliny, in writing to Trajan (98–117), implies that he has not witnessed any trial of Christians, though he imposed death on any who would not renounce Christ by invoking the Roman gods and sacrificing to a statue of the emperor. One historian comments:

> There is no evidence that imperial officials sponsored systematic or widespread persecution of Jesus' followers for the rest of the first century or well into the second ... The arrest and execution of Bishop Ignatius of Antioch and the tribulation inspiring the Book of Revelation, around the end of the first century, appear to be isolated incidents. (Daniel Schowalter in Coogan, 1998: 388–419, 403)

Christians in Corinth

The best way to get a picture of Christians in a Roman City is to describe one city. We choose Corinth (Crossan and Reed 2005: 293–99; Meeks, 1983: 47–49).

First century Corinth was a city whose life was determined by various factors of its situation and groups within its different geographical areas:
1. As a travel centre – sea and land, so provision for visitors and overnights.
2. As a commercial centre – Corinth was strategically placed to link the Aegean and the Adriatic. It was a major junction between east and west. Corinth had two sea ports. Ships from the East docked at Cenchrae, from where their cargoes were taken to Lechaion, to go north.
3. As a centre for certain local trades, including agriculture and crafts. There were many orchards and vineyards along the fertile coastal region.
4. As a Greek city, including libraries and temples. It was a classical city in every sense, with bathing, exercise and dining facilities.
5. As a Roman administrative centre, including forum and coliseum. It was rebuilt in 44 BCE by Julius Caesar. In 27 BCE, it became the capital and administrative centre for the Roman province of Achaia. Corinth's Acropolis – the Acrocorinth – dominated the city from the south, with two large forums, and rows of shops.
6. As a place of rich and prominent people, living in town houses or country villas. Corinth was a major cosmopolitan centre. The Agora

had temples to Apollo, Tyche, Venus and Hera, and the twin goddesses of fertility, Demeter and Kore.

7. As a place of many cultures from outside (including Jews), which each had their quarter.

8. As a city with a large slave population living in tenements. These large buildings were separate from the central complex.

The architecture and city planning reflect this variety of interests and occupations.

The tiny Christian groups belong to three of the eight situations and groups:

1. a few rich Gentile patrons, who used their homes;
2. some Jews and Proselytes; and
3. slaves – from the patrons' homes(?).

The Social Stratification of the Corinthian Community is clear:

> Consider your own call, brothers and sisters: not many of you were wise by human standards, not many were powerful, not many were of noble birth. But God chose what is foolish in the world to shame the wise; God chose what is weak in the world to shame the strong; God chose what is low and despised in the world, things that are not, to reduce to nothing things that are, so that no one might boast in the presence of God. God is the source of your life in Christ Jesus, who became for us wisdom from God, and righteousness and sanctification and redemption, in order that, as it is written, Let the one who boasts, boast in the Lord. (1Cor. 1:26–29)

The contrasts between those "of noble birth", which are repeated in vv. 27–28, with "nothing people", or "despised people", or "lower-born people" are all used in Plato, Euripides, Sophocles and Philo to denote a superior person's view of those "at the bottom" (Theissen, 1982: 70–72).

Clearly, there are both "high" and "low" Christians in Corinth. Indeed, the "high" people are apparently those for whom Paul has some contempt:

> We are fools for Christ – you are clever in Christ.
> We are weak – you are strong.
> We are held in contempt – you in honour. (1Cor. 4:10)

Also, there were people of high office in the Christian churches. Some were called *oikonomos*, like Erastus, the city treasurer (Rom. 16:23), though this was "a low-level financial bureaucrat", usually a slave, following the Vulgate translation (Theissen 1982: 76).

The House (*oikos*) of Stephanas (1 Cor. 1:16) and the House (*oikio*) (1 Cor. 16:15) indicates a person giving himself to the community's service. Stephanas and his friends refreshed Paul's spirit (1 Cor. 16:18). Phoebe

(Rom. 16:1) helped Paul and others in whatever *pragma*, business, she required (1 Cor. 16:2). Christians are to support her, as she supports them.

Providing hospitality for Paul and others was another way for the more well-to-do to help. Theissen lists all those who carried out three decisive tasks:

1. provided houses;
2. provided services; and
3. travelled.

Theissen concludes: "of the seventeen persons (including one group) listed, nine belong to the upper classes" (Theissen, 1982: 94–95).

How different these "wise" or "upper class" were is disputed. Justin Meggitt writes:

> It may be that the few wise, powerful, and well-born were a small group of literate, *ingénue*, artisans – who amongst the urban poor would have appeared relatively more privileged but whose lives would still have been dominated by fears over subsistence. Indeed, it is probable that, in absolute terms, the gap between the *sophos*, *dunatos* and *eugenes* and the rest of the congregation was not very great: the apostle soon forgets the distinction that he has drawn and refers to *all* of the Corinthian community, *all* of the called, in the subsequent two verses, as foolish, weak, low, despised nothings. (Meggitt, 1998: 106).

Meggit thus questions whether Theissen is right that there are two different socio-economic groups, with some "elevated" people in the church.

The tiny Christian community had to preserve its own identity in the midst of this great Roman city. The Epistle describes some of the problems which the Christians faced, partly no doubt because of their context. 1 Corinthians refers to factions (1:10–17), incest (5:1–5), lawsuits (6:1–8), immorality (6:12–20), marital issues (7:1–9), food offered to idols (8:1–13), women's attire in worship (11:2–16), behaviour at the Lord's Supper (11:17–33), excesses in expressing *pneumata* (12–14) and disagreements over resurrection (15).

The influence of the city's style is seen in 1 Corinthians 1–4, particularly in relation to secular customs of discipleship and competitiveness. The Corinthians were "operating in a secular fashion" (3:3) because they compared Paul and Apollos and possibly Peter with one another in the same way that secular disciples did with their teachers and fellow students. In a city such as Corinth, pupils and teachers had very strong and exclusive relationships, and there was great competitiveness between teachers. The merits of one teacher were played off against those of another by their respective pupils (Winter, 2001: 31–39).

There is also in Corinth a conflict regarding the way in which one should live. The lifestyle of Paul is depicted in 1 Corinthians 4:8–13 as a deliberate contrast to that of the upper class disciples – full, rich, living like kings (v.8). Paul describes his lifestyle as a "self-lowering" (Horrell, 1996: 202), even to "labouring with our hands".

> Paul's insistence on supporting himself in part through his own labour not only portrays him as someone of lower social status (and thus as a less worthy leader, to some) but who also becomes a particular cause of conflict between him and some of the Corinthians.

His manual work is "part of a conscious decision to reject financial support from certain members of the Corinthian congregation", and "a means of identifying and siding with the weak" (Horrell, 1996: 203). Again, the table practice urged by Paul in 1 Corinthians 11:17–34 challenged head-on the patronal society, where the poor came only after the rich had eaten, with the Christian model of an egalitarian "shared meal" (Crossan 1998: 423–44; Horrell, 1996: 203).

> Especially and maybe even uniquely at Corinth, Paul's radical horizontal Christian equality clashed forcibly with Roman society's normal vertical hierarchy. (Crossan and Reed, 2005: 296)

Paul and Home

As we have seen, in rural areas such as Capernaum (p. 59), the "four-room house" had three long rooms in a U-shape around a central common courtyard with, on the fourth side, a wall and gate. Elsewhere in the Roman empire, the Greek "peristyle house" is like the four-room house, but has a covered courtyard ambulatory. Such houses are found in Sepphoris and many other cities like Pergamon and Ephesus. When more rooms were added, the building became a "terraced house". Other small houses, with smaller rooms, were built above shops or workshops, often having additional floors for bedrooms. A complex of several houses is the "insula" houses and shops preserved in the house of the Bicentenary at Herculaneum, Pompeii, preserved exactly by the volcanic eruption of Vesuvius in 67 CE.

More affluent houses in Ephesus and elsewhere had more space and more rooms, often with an atrium, plus bathrooms and central heating. Walls were decorated elaborately, and mosaics were on the floors, as in the triclinium mosaic floor of the Sepphoris villa, with Dionysiac emblems.

It would certainly make more sense if the woman who enters a banquet where Jesus was a guest, in Luke 7:6–50, was entering a Roman-style triclinium, where Jesus and the others are reclining with their feet away from the central table. Front doors appear to have been left open during dinner, so that the woman could gain entry – like the "outsider" in 1 Corinthians 14:6.

The Insula at Herculaneum indicates the architectural and social relationships between house, apartment and shop. Several adjacent doors lead to shops. A larger door is the main entrance to the villa, and others open on to stairs leading to upstairs apartments (Crossan and Reed, 2005: 320–23). Seventeen wooden tablets of several waxed sheets each tell the story of the intricate relationships in a single extended family between the husband, wife and child, and the freeborn, freed and slaves (Crossan and Reed, 2005: 322–23; Andrew Wallace-Hadrill in Balch and Osiek, 2003, 3–18).

Most urban dwellers, however, lived in large apartment houses, multiple-unit tenement blocks, which Augustus limited to 70 ft high (21 m), and Trajan after him to 60 ft (18 m). Such tenements varied from the luxurious to the most squalid.

In Corinth, Paul worked in the tentmaking business of Priscilla and Aquila (Acts 18:2). They also had a house church (1 Corinthians 16:19). Their shop or workshop could have had a storey above, with a guest room and apartment in it. If this is the case, the house-church could have met in the shop/workshop. However, if, as 1 Corinthians implies, there were also rich people in the house church, it could have met in the larger room of the villa of which the shop/workshop is a part. Only there would have been space and furnishings to suit the two-group assembly implied in 1 Corinthians 11:17–34. The shop/workshop would be run by the slaves, freedmen, freedwomen and dependants of the villa family.

Paul insisted on everyone being the same, especially "slaves or free" (1 Cor. 12:13). Were the few "high born" of 1 Corinthians 1:26 continuing conventional patronage relationships? Did Paul's coming "in weakness, fear and trembling" (1 Cor. 2:2), meant to mirror the radical self-giving of Jesus, only lead others to conclude: "his bodily presence is weak, and his speech contemptible" (2 Cor. 10:10)? Right, says Paul, "whenever I am weak, then I am strong" (2 Cor. 12:10), and lists his dangers and hardships (2 Cor. 11:23–33) as evidence of his being a servant (*diakonos*) of Christ (2 Cor. 11:23).

In terms of city life, the "high born" were powerful people, who were accustomed to determining who could marry whom (1 Cor. 5:1–13), what should be done with money (6:1–8), and what you could eat at banquets

(10:14–33). The ordinary members, slaves or freed, could not settle any of these things.

Churches in Houses

House churches and the names of their hosts occur frequently (Meeks, 1983: 75–80; Osiek in Hill, 1998: 300–15). "The brothers who are with them" or "The saints who are with them" means those who are in their house church. House churches are mentioned at Philippi (Acts 16:40), Corinth (Acts 18:7), Rome (Rom. 16:5, 14, 15), Ephesus (1 Cor. 16:19), Laodicea (Col. 4:15) and Colossae (Phil. 1:2). Some traditions have the upper room of Mk 14:14–15 and Lk. 22:11–13 as the same as "the upper room where they were staying" of Acts 1:12, 13, though that had room for 120 (Acts 1:15). Some have linked this with "the house of Mary, the mother of John, whose other name was Mark" (Acts 12:12).

A house church might have consisted solely of the members of the household, as perhaps with the baptized households of Stephanus (1 Cor. 1:16; 16:15), Cornelius (Acts 10:2, 44–48), Lydia (Acts 16:14–15, 40), and the jailer (Acts 16:31–33). Other house churches met in the homes of Prisca and Aquila (1 Cor. 16; Rom. 16:3–5), Philemon, Apphia and Archippos (Phlm 1), possibly Mary, the mother of John Mark (Acts 12:12) and also Nympha (Col. 4:15). The owner of the house in which the small community met was usually the leader of the group as well as its patron, and thus should be respected and followed, as with Stephanus (1 Cor. 16:15–16).

We assume the identification of the bread and wine commemorative meal of the Last Supper with the "breaking of bread in each other's homes" of the early church. But this is far from clear. Sharing meals was in itself a characteristic of the Jesus movement. Just as the meals of Jesus and his disciples represented and helped create the alternative Israel community during his own ministry, so also in the early church there were plenty of traditions embodying the idea of religious meals taken together by fellow-religionists, which had either no or questionable connections to any ideas of ritual sacrifice. As models for the Christian sharing meals, the Jewish religious meetings for study and meal sharing – the *chaburah* – thus have their counterpart in the *symposium* of Greco-Roman religions (Smith, 2003: 12–131).

Regarding 1 Corinthians 11:17–34, Carolyn Osiek describes the problem thus, assuming the meetings were in a typical peristyle house:

The meal seems not to be supplied by the patron in whose house they meet, but by different people bringing food, after the model of a *thiasos* or religious association meeting. However, the seating arrangement probably remains the same as that of the patronage model of hospitality, whereby the host leaders and most distinguished guests or community members reclined in the triclinium while everyone else either reclined or sat on movable couches or tables or chairs within hearing of those in the triclinium. It is likely that the séance of prayer, prophecy, and tongues described in 1 Cor. 14 is the second part of the supper, following the model of the symposium with eating first and discussion or entertainment afterward, rather than a distinct meeting. 1 Cor. 14:30 implies that most in attendance were sitting rather than reclining and that this is a rather freely structured session in which anyone can rise and speak. (Osiek in Blasi *et al.*, 2002: 83–103, 99).

The 1 Corinthians 14 worship model would work equally well for the living-room of a tenement room or a shop.

Equality

In Philemon, Paul tells a slave-owner to welcome back his runaway slave as "a beloved brother" (Phlm 15). In 1 Corinthians 7, Paul emphasizes the mutuality of husband and wife in all things. In 1 Corinthians 11:3–16, Paul argues that men and women are equal "in the Lord". In each of the seven genuine letters, Paul names 27 people, of whom ten are women, as "deacon" or "apostle" or "hard worker". His list of "gifts" in Romans 12:6–8 covers all classes and both sexes, the more socially elevated roles of donor, patron and generous person coming after the more pastoral roles of prophecy, *diakonia*, teacher and exhorter. Paul thus stresses equalities in family, assembly and apostolate (Crossan and Reed, 2005: 107–20; Peter Lampe in Balch and Osiek, 2003: 73–83).

However, the Christian view of equality conflicted with the current practice in the city, in at least three major matters: those concerning women, slaves and status.

Women

There is at present a lively debate on how far women were prominent in early Christian groups. Robin Lane Fox argues that "Christian women were prominent in the churches' membership and recognised to be so by Christians and pagans" (Fox, 1987: 308). Judith Lieu sees a novelistic style in the stories of Lydia (Acts 16:11–15) and the noblewomen of Thessalonica (Acts 17:4, 12; cf. 17:33–34), and concludes:

> The gendering of conversion is a matter of rhetorical and not of statistical analysis. The move from rhetoric to social experience must remain hazardous (Lieu, 1998: 16–19).

However, others point out that some women were clearly important. Prisca is both house church leader (1Cor. 16:19; Rom. 16:3–5) and evangelist (Acts 18:24–26). Teams of two women – Euodia and Syntyche (Phil. 4:2–3) and Tryphena and Tryphosa (Rom. 16:12) – engage in apostolic work. The notable husband-and-wife team Prisca/Priscilla and Aquila make one wonder:

> Could the household base of the mission of Prisca and Aquila have meant that Prisca actually was a more influential missioner than her partner? (Margaret Macdonald in Balch and Osiek, 2003: 157–84, 166; Crossan, 2007: 177–79)

Her name certainly comes first in Romans 16:3 and Acts 1:18, 26. And women are described as sister, deacon, co-worker (so Phoebe, Rom. 16:1–2) and apostle (so Junia, Rom. 16:7) in Paul's letters. This open opportunity for women as travellers and evangelists was curtailed in the later Pseudo-Pauline letters, which emphasized the family (e.g. Eph. 3:14–15; 5:22–23). Probably also, in the later first century, marriages of Christian women with non-Christian husbands might have been less frequent (Macdonald in Balch and Osiek, 2003: 175–81).

Slaves

Paul's list of the "not many wise by earthly standards, or powerful or nobly born" (1 Cor. 1:26) in the early church, followed by his list of those whom God has actually chosen – low, contemptible, nonentities (v. 28) – are actually the people who are those who even now "overthrow the existing order" (v. 28). The promise of Jesus that "the first shall be last, and the last shall be first" (Mk 10:31, etc.) is actually realized in the character and activity of the early believers. In Romans, Abraham is a model not for "success" but for God's "calling things into existence that do not exist" (Rom. 4:17).

The Christian community of "saints" belonging to "the household of Caesar" who are greeted by Paul from gaol in Philippians 4:22 could have been in Rome itself, or in Ephesus or Caesarea. This *familia* could have been imperial slaves or freedmen, and could have been important state officials or domestic workers. But being in Caesar's household would have given anyone the chance to mix widely and become upwardly mobile.

As well as slaves, there were slave-owners who were Christians – Philemon and Apphia certainly, and Chloe probably. "Chloe's people"

(1 Cor. 1:11) would be slaves or former slaves. A slave's attitude is used as an illustration in 1 Corinthians 7:20–24.

As in many other ways, the later letters attributed to Paul but probably not written by him – Ephesians, Colossians, 2 Thessalonians, 1 and 2 Timothy and Titus – move in a much more conservative direction. Here, the common Hellenistic moral codes or "House Rules" (*Haustafeln*) are repeated as appropriate also for Christians. Colossians 3:22–25 instructs slaves specifically, as does its parallel in Ephesians 6:5–8. Women's equality is denied in Colossians 3:18–4.1, Ephesians 5:22–6:9 and I Timothy 2:8–15, besides the questionably Pauline 1 Corinthians 14:33b–36 (Crossan and Reed, 2005: 110–20).

Status
Equality for the rich or privileged, according to Paul, implies being alongside the poor. The "journey downwards" which Paul, as an educated Pharisee, makes when he undertakes work in tent-making may have its origin in the custom that rabbis always had a trade – or equally in the decisions of rhetoricians and philosophers from higher social levels who decide to do menial work (Hook, 1980: 65). Clearly, this intentional policy gives Paul an independent work style, rejecting patronage. The generosity of Jesus who "was rich, yet for your sake became poor" (2 Cor. 8:9) may be based on the similar journey by Jesus in his own life, opting for a costly ministry among the poor, and himself becoming poor. An "option for the poor" results as a characteristic of Christian vocation, based on the self-sacrificial life practice of Greek teachers mirrored in the lives of both Jesus and Paul. Such a chosen lower social position is also indicated if Paul's tent shop became a centre for his congregational or evangelistic work, as was the famous Cobbler's shop of Simon the Cynic philosopher (Hook, 1980: 37–42).

Getting rid of some of the advantages of education and wealth are part of the renunciation of the "sophistries and sources of pride" that prevent one appearing weak and foolish so that God's wisdom might come through (2 Cor. 10:3–6; 17–18). In any case, "giving up" is what God accepts (2 Cor. 8:12), and it will lead, without hardship to ourselves, to coming nearer to equality (2 Cor. 8:13).

Such motivations for intentional vocational and gospel-based movement downwards within the structures of society imply a very conscious attempt to take seriously what one's chosen place in society says in terms of one's political, social and civic commitment and message. Paul's complaint against the wise, strong and well-born is basically that they stay as they are, and will not move towards becoming less wise, weaker and more equal with others – and these are precisely the characteristics which Paul wishes to be adopted through an assimilation to Christ. "Follow my example, as I follow Christ's" (1 Cor. 11:1) does not refer to internal or spiritual intentions, but to what one does in practical witness in the spheres of society, culture and politics continuing Christ's self-emptying (Phil. 2:5–8).

The classic "evangelical counsels" of chastity, obedience and poverty in the later monastic orders provided three disciplines not totally unlike the early Christian practice with regard to women, slaves and status. And the radical Christian tradition has seen all three elements as crucial civic and political tools in the creation of significant contextual parabolic action in the city.

Relation to Authorities

In the ordinary life of the city, customary rules of decent and responsible behaviour are repeated:

> We urge you to try to live quietly, to mind your own affairs, and to work with your hands, as we directed you, so that you appear properly behaved in the view of outsiders, and are not dependent on others. (1 Thess. 4:11–12)

Excesses in worship are to be avoided, lest visitors think members possessed or insane (1 Cor. 14:23).

Regarding one's suggested attitude to the state, Romans 13:1 stands alone:

> Let every person be subject to the governing authorities. For there is no authority except from God, and existing authorities have been instituted by God. Resistance against authorities is resistance against God.

Only in this one place in the authentic Pauline letters is there explicit reference to political authorities. Most interpreters see in Romans 13:1–7 the standard guidelines formulated by Jewish diaspora communities, primarily intended to avoid the authorities instigating or permitting any anti-Jewish activity, such as occurred with regular intervals in many cities. Wayne Meeks comments on Romans 13:

> The picture of the state is idealized in this context, but the experience of urban Jesus on numerous occasions indicated the advocacy of this ideal as their best policy, and the Pauline Christians followed their example. (Meeks, 1983: 106)

Thus, though Paul constantly emphasizes the "new existence" within which there is neither Jew nor Greek, the reality is that Paul's experience and that of his mainly ex-Jewish or ex-proselyte communities was that they were not in any position to take up political attitudes to the State, but had to "keep their heads down" so that the State would not notice them. In this respect, as in many others, it suited the nascent Christian communities to appear in the public realm as neo-Judaistic groups, only distinguishable from other Judaistic groups by their open-handed and (circumcision condition free) welcome to pagans.

The relation to authorities which Paul and the congregations of the early church adopted was determined by pragmatic necessities. This apparent attitude of subservience to authorities may be part of a wider argument of Paul, who throughout Romans is exposing the Roman civic cult and the Roman system as a pagan counterweight to Israel's history. Rome is dethroned if God is establishing rulers:

> That Roman authorities were ordained by the God and Father of Jesus Christ turns the entire Roman civic cult on its head, exposing its suppression of the truth. (Robert Jewett in Horsley, 2000: 58–71, 66).

The passage is a radical claim that the whole Roman system of gods and emperor-gods is not valid. The God of Jesus alone "appoints". Whatever he claims, the emperor "remains answerable to the true God", and "reminding the emperor's subjects that the emperor is responsible to the true God is a diminution of, not a subjection to, imperial arrogance" (N. T. Wright in Horsley, 2000: 160–83, 172). As for Christian obedience, it is not a passive, subordinate stance. Rather, it is the powerful stance of active *agapé*:

> Do not be indebted to anyone for anything, except for the mutual obligation of mutual *agape*. For the one who is loving to others has achieved everything in the law. (Rom. 13:8)

Apart from this, Roman power is highly temporary. All things, including Rome, are coming to an end. God's kingdom will replace the Roman kingdom, as Romans 13:11–12 makes clear. Then what God is *really* ordaining will become plain.

However one views Romans 13:1–7, it clearly cannot be taken over as a policy good for all time.

Chapter 7

PERSPECTIVES FOR OUR CITIES

Coherence with God's Project

The existence today of "the global city" presents new challenges (Green, 2001; Davey, 2002; Commission on Urban Life, 2006: 36–37). Britain belongs to "the global market", and everything we do is influenced by that fact. Our cities are merely the local manifestations of global realities.

The New Testament is precisely about an alternative globalization Project, which is "God's Project". In Jesus's day, the global system was the Roman Empire, with its head and "first man", Caesar Augustus, who was Son of God, Saviour and Prince of Peace. Jesus's claim was that there was now an alternative global system, the Kingdom of Heaven on Earth, and his followers championed its own "first man", the man Jesus of Nazareth, claimed also to be Son of God, Saviour and Prince of Peace.

New Testament discipleship, ethics, Christology and theology are all based on the prime question: How can I, who am now a citizen of this new Kingdom of God present on earth, survive as a counter-cultural community, and be prophetic and redemptive for the whole world, while I am still living in a world totally dominated by the powers of Rome, plus the controlling forces of my previous religion, be it Jewish or pagan?

Certainly, the New Testament witnesses would have great difficulty with many churches today, which preach, practise and represent to others a Christianity of personal, family and Christian group piety and responsibility, but simply recognizing the legitimacy of the globalization situation. City discipleship appears just to be good behaviour or generous living lived by those otherwise in every way living off globalization and its benefits.

As we have seen, the Project of God is, in both Jesus and Paul, that disciples are called to be part of a new creation, which is God's present Realm, which takes symbolic and prophetic form within each varying time, society and culture. So we must ask: What is the dynamic of this Kingdom in our globalization situation? What do we do when "The pursuit of prosperity risks creating such an acquisitive global society that the only values that count are profit, power and status" (Commission on Urban Life, 2006: 37)? How can we be disciples of a new creation, which is "in but not of" the globalization project? Does this mean we search out or create attitudes, lifestyles, policies, projects, places and communities which are post-globalization, or post-capitalist? Or, if not everywhere doing that, then where, in what, and how can we be para-globalization people, para-capitalist people? Does the concept of "alongside" have anything to offer – whom can we actively be "alongside" today (Vincent, 2000: 100–10)?

Even the great virtues which Christians share with most religions – and humanism – such as truth, justice, shalom, freedom, responsibility and equality, represent totally different realities when looked at within the globalization project, or outside or alongside it.

Is Christianity then a counter-culture? It has become fashionable recently for church leaders to raise the possibility that Christianity might have to become a counter-cultural movement (so Archbishop Rowan Williams in recent media comments).

However, the choice of being or becoming counter-cultural has to be based on the assumption or the argument, preferably also the experience, that what we have or what we think we could have are so significant and determinative for us that they do in fact constitute a definite and specifically different "culture". Is that the case with most of what passes for Christianity in Britain today?

Actually, the New Testament does not speak of "culture". It speaks of "the *nous* that was in Christ", or "the *logos* that becomes human", or "God's heaven now on earth", or "the new creation", or "the Alpha and the Omega". The decisive question has to be: Where and how, in what particulars, in what practice, in what communities, have we in Christianity today got anything remotely like the phenomenon or phenomena that the first Christians had when they coined phrases like these to describe their reality?

Of course, the early Christians would admit, "We use these cosmic, global, eternal descriptions for our reality, even though it and we are very tiny, very specific, very local". Precisely so. Therefore, we have to ask, Where, today, are there traces of such reality? In what particulars do or could we in our city practice today "cohere with God's Project"?

One has to observe that none of the Churches' reports on the city, *Faith in the City* (1985), *The Cities* (1997) and *Faithful Cities* (2006) use Gospel or New Testament models for practice to any great extent. *Faith in the City* works from Paul's "Remember the poor" (Gal. 2:10). *The Cities* has a model of Creation, Incarnation, Cross and Resurrection and Pilgrimage. *Faithful Cities* generally adopts a Eucharistic theological model (Vincent, 2010: forthcoming).

Making Connections

The modern disciple or disciple community seeking for ways to connect the New Testament witnesses to their own options today is faced with a two-fold opportunity:

1. Are there specific incidents, passages, emphases, anywhere in all this which call forth resonances with our life now?
2. Is there a dominant tradition which should inform our attitude and policy in civil life and politics?

Methods of Connection

At the "Bible and the City" MA Module in Spring 2008 at the Urban Theology Unit, the group produced this list of the grounds they had found which led to making connections between biblical scenarios or themes and their own experiences or concerns:

Small town ethos	Group in Society
Violence	Deviance
Dramatic incident	Occupation
Relationships	Daily life ritual
Psychological	Responses to God
Parallel experience	Reactive/contrary

Each reader and each group should ask what in themselves and in a biblical piece feels to have a resonance or relationship. The traditions in Matthew and Luke of Christian disciples both building up their own alternative community and also engaging significantly with the surrounding community (pp. 77–79) are very relevant here.

This method of "imaginative identification" allows us to envisage and expand our work in the city by the scheme of "moves" outlined by Norman Gottwald (pp. 102–05). It has been used in many contexts, especially in the life of Christian urban communities and in urban ministry projects (Duffield in Vincent, 2003: 226–79).

Dominant Traditions

Here we may identify at least four major perspectives, which are ways in which connections can be made between "God's Project" and the existing society, in different situations.

1. Jesus: Embodiment

The dominant concern of Jesus and of Paul and the early Church is to set up wherever possible and in whatever possible ways a parallel society which embodies the values and life of the Kingdom of God, here on earth. Under this heading, all that we have discovered about this "Alternative city" in Chapter 5, pp. 68–70, comes into play. The overall Christian civic policy derives from two major paradigms:

1. Jesus was engaged in rebuilding and revitalizing communities in their fundamental socio-economic relations as the constructive aspect of the now present kingdom of God.
2. Paul was making Jesus the head of an anti-imperial international alternative society.

In light of this, the fundamental calling of the Christian community is to be a relevant, secular, embodied manifestation on the streets of the new reality present on earth, the Kingdom of God (Michael Northcott in Vincent, 2003: 244–65). Today, disciples "make connections" with the ways this was embodied in New Testament times.

2. Jesus: Subversion

The key text is Mark 12:13–17.

> If it has Caesar's inscription on it, give it to Caesar.
> If it has God's inscription on it, give it to God.

It is Jesus's clever way out of being put on the spot by a questioner. If he had said that you should not pay the Roman tax (Caesar's), the Romans could have arrested him. If he had said don't pay the temple tax (God's), the temple authorities could have accused him. He makes a joke of it. Look at the coin in your hand, and use it for Rome if it is a Roman coin, for the temple if it is a temple coin (Myers, 1988: 312–14).

It is a totally evasive answer – like most of Jesus's answers in Mark 10–12. It can only mean that it is a matter of indifference to the new community of the Kingdom of heaven on earth whether you happen to be cornered by Roman rules or by Temple rules. Just play it safe, as neither is a vital matter. Is it indifference? Or is it a subtle way of subverting both Rome and Temple? The violent man looks silly if you offer him the other cheek (Mt. 5:38). The enforcer is embarrassed if you offer to carry his pack a second mile (Mt. 5:41).

The task in the city today, then, on this view, is to find ways to embody a politics and a community which as far as possible keeps you out of unnecessary trouble but inwardly subverts the authorities, and tries to pioneer an alternative society, and meanwhile live differently (Timothy Gorringe in Rowland and Vincent, 2001: 44–49).

3. Paul: Compliance

The key text is the problematic Romans 13: 1–2.

> Existing authorities are set there by God. And to disobey them is to disobey God.

Apart from the questionable origin of the statements (see p. 94), we would simply have to observe that if Paul was imprisoned and/or executed in Rome by the authorities, as some suggest, then he would hardly have kept this view. In any case, he does not himself carry out this mandate.

Karl Wengst writes:

> Paul admonishes his readers not to resist the political powers with which even Christians have to deal, but to give them what they demand: taxes, duties, reverence and respect. (Wengst, 1987: 83)

In this way, Paul merely repeats common Jewish attitudes, such as the oath of the Essenes according to Josephus: "Always to be loyal to all, but especially to the authorities, since no one has a position of rule apart from God" (*Bell. Jud.* II, 140). But Paul's use of "God's agents" (three times) and "God's service" (once) for political powers is still problematic (Neil Elliott in Horsley, 2000: 17–39, 38–39).

On this model, Christians in the city comply with civic laws without questioning them. However, through history, Romans 13 has been a disastrous doctrine. Consequently, it has been advocated by Christians or churches which happened to be able to connive with a powerful state. Equally consistently, it has been opposed or ignored by Christians when the state persecuted or opposed them.

4. Revelation: Replacement

Perhaps around 120 CE, John of Patmos tries to counter a vicious and bloody persecution of Christians by giving the churches an apocalyptic vision of a future world in which the oppressors themselves would be exterminated. The state has revealed itself as God's ultimate enemy – the whore of Babylon. It is exterminating the people of God. But now, in a vision, John sees the state punished for its opposition to God.

The vision of the heavenly Jerusalem in Revelation 21:10–27 is not very useful – it is purely a non-material construction, a "counterpart" to Rome, which uses for itself all the images of Rome the harlot (Crossan, 2007:

191–235; Wengst, 1987: 129–131). In any case, it is only one picture alongside others of the future condition which God will establish to replace the state. Whether and when this is to happen on the physical earth has been debated endlessly. Christians have used the images *in extremis* when all hope for a reformed earthly city has disappeared.

Christians today, as in every age, have to decide their own points of connection with the (at least) four options taken by the first Christians.

"Making Connections"

The basic idea in this series "Biblical Challenges in the Contemporary World" is that there are important things that we can learn in dealing with our modern issues that we can discern from the Bible. That means that we today, from our own situations and practice, might consider some biblical situations and practices that might help us. So, we seek to "make connections" between our situation and a biblical one.

There are a number of ways in which we can "make connections" between texts and ourselves.

Initially, as already indicated (p. 76), we need to make some realistic "Situation Analysis" of ourselves. Only then can we see some of the interests that we ourselves carry to the text.

A famous modern Old Testament scholar, Norman Gottwald, suggests that we need to follow three "Movements with Texts", three stages in a "hermeneutical appropriation".

> First, the "Move" from my Situation to the Text.
> Second, the "Movement" within the Text (Exegesis Proper).
> Third, the "Move" from the Text's "Movement" back to My Situation. (Gottwald in Vincent, 2006: 15–17; also Davies and Vincent in Vincent, 2006: 17–22)

1. The Move from My Situation to the Text
In examining whether we can make a connection between myself and/or my community, we need to do what is often called a "Situation Analysis".

Here, we need to look at questions like:

The area
1. The area – is it a city, a town, a village, an estate, an inner city?
2. The neighbourhood – what is near us: shops, schools, places of worship, houses?

3. What goes on locally – community life, events, ethos, view of place by outsiders?
4. The Church Community – how does it relate to 1, 2 and 3?

The people
1. Who are they? Elderly, middle aged, young families, children, single?
2. What sort of jobs do they have? Where do they work?
3. Why are they here? Degrees of choice or coercion. Where do they come from?
4. How long have they been here? Stability/mobility?

Social analysis
These questions are followed by others relating to relationships between people, perceptions of the area from inside and outside, and recent experiences within the local community. Lifestyle questions are pressed to get elements of "Social Analysis":
1. What conflicts of lifestyle are there in the community?
2. What assumptions and values are indicated by the way groups of people live?
3. Are there "top" people and "bottom" people? When it comes to the crunch, whose side are you on?

Structural analysis
Our situation thus involves us in a whole series of intricate behaviour patterns, relationships, power-plays and stances. Behind them are wider questions of "Structural Analysis", like – How does the reality we experience locally form a part of the economic, social, administrative and political reality of the area and the country as a whole (Holland and Henriot, 1983: 98–100)?

These are the kinds of "connections" we are looking for. Obviously, the biblical situation is very different from ours. But there must be some factors which make us think there is a connection or connections.

Norman Gottwald suggests that we do some reflection before we make "The Move from My Situation to the Text":

Why do I choose this text, theme or socio-religious situation instead of others? Have I adequately considered other options? Have I made sufficient use of biblical reference works to canvas these opinions? Have I considered what appeals to Scripture are made by theological/ethical works that treat "my situation" most relevantly? Should I use already "tried and true" texts, or venture into fresh textual resources, thematic possibilities, and socio-religious contexts? Am I prepared to abandon a false or abortive start when the text or theme or biblical period do not speak to the problem that I first thought they did? (Gottwald in Vincent, 2006: 15)

2. The Movement within the Text

If we are going to make connections with a Biblical passage, we need to carry out the same kind of Situation Analysis of the characteristics of the passage as we do for our own situation. As Gottwald says:

> It is necessary to press the written text back into *somebody's experience* in a situation that was problematic, promising, threatening for the speaker-writer and for *some community*. Text is not mere disembodied word, but a speaking from out of someone's situation which *may* have one or another analogy with the interpreter's situation. (Gottwald in Vincent, 2006: 16)

So, we are looking for people in a biblical situation who were dealing with certain issues or threats which, when we analyse them in socio-political, economic, and even relational terms, seem to have some connection with the issues or threats that we face.

Here, Gottwald sees two aspects to what happens when an individual or a group deals with a piece of biblical material – a text, a theme, a motif, or a socio-religious situation.

> 1. There is the movement of the text's own internal life, both as a literary composition of a certain genre and as an expression of a response to a situation. This movement will connect and contrast in varying ways with earlier/later/similar/dissimilar texts.
> 2. There is the movement that I as an exegete must go through in order to penetrate the text's distinctive movement. Exegesis provides for a number of "fixes" or "checks" on the text. Often called "exegetical steps", their exact sequence is less important than that they all receive consideration as of relevance to an understanding of the text. (Gottwald in Vincent, 2006: 16)

These "fixes" or "checks" on the text deal especially with "the language of symbolism" and "the socio-economic-political issues", which help our understanding of the biblical situations, "just as I have striven to understand my own situation in terms of the latest analytic resources".

3. The Move Back to my Situation

As we observed earlier, the "connection" might prove to be "false or abortive", "if the text or theme of Biblical period do not speak to the problem that I first thought they did".

But, assuming that we have seen the characteristics of our own situation realistically, and done the same with a biblical piece, then the "cargo"

I bring back will be significant – though probably not exactly what we had expected when we began our biblical journey.

In this move back to our own situation, of course, the results will depend very largely upon what our situation is.

Thus, if we are a student of biblical texts, or are busy with an essay or article, getting material together, we will deal with a number of questions like:

- How can I best describe, in my own contemporary terms, what I have discovered in this biblical material?
- What specific elements in this biblical material resonate with or conflict with issues coming from wider biblical perspectives or interpretations?
- What theological or ideological conclusions, if any, do I bring back from this study?

We could also be a reader opening this book as part of a search for contemporary discipleship, or a member of a group studying scripture as part of a community search for contemporary mission. Our questions would then be like these:

- What are the "spin-offs" for my vocation or our vocation?
- What are the mandates, implications, applications for our practice today?
- What affect is this Bible study going to have on our church's programme? Does it support us, criticize us, offer us new suggestions for action? (John Davies and Vincent in Vincent, 2006: 21).

The stages of our "making connections" can be summarized as:

1. Choose a passage that seems to make some sense to you in your context.
2. Do an exegesis of the passage in the light of your context.
3. Do an exegesis of your context in the light of the passage.

Coherence with God's Project

"Making Connections" is designed to land us within a world of imagination and transformation, in which we dialogue with situation – relevant, biblical partners, seeking compatible biblical practice today. But the practice also has to deal with another larger issue. Both Old and New Testaments have a wider perspective than single context-related pieces of action. Both Testaments also have what can only be described as over-arching themes, concerns and purposes, which can be described as "God's Project" – what God is trying to do, which thus determines what faith, trust, action and commitment to God means for human beings.

Coherence with God's Project in the Old Testament would mean the attempt in differing circumstances to give present reality to the concerns of Yahweh in the Old Testament. Walter Brueggemann describes God's Project with Israel (and us) as:

> Yahweh's passion for justice, passion for the well-being of the human community, and passion for the *shalom* of the earth ... [that] refuses to come to terms with the power of death, no matter its particular public form or its ideological garb. (Brueggemann, 1997: 741)

Thus any reading or practice which does not cohere with the divine passions for the well-being of the human community and the *shalom* of the earth is not coherent with God's Project. And any reading or practice that reflects these divine passions is indeed coherent with God's Project. So that *any* project, be it civic, national, social or ecclesial, has to pass this "test" of the divine passions. So, of the Old Testament testimony:

> From the outset, it is operative in the world of power, and it concerns the rise and fall of empires and the living and dying of human persons and communities. (Brueggemann, 1997: 113)

In the New Testament, God's Project becomes focused in the person and work of Jesus centred upon acting out the presence of the Kingdom of Heaven/God here on earth. Jesus's Project is thus to celebrate "God's Kingdom come" and "God's will being done" on earth. As we have seen, the Kingdom's presence means, in Jesus's terms, for himself, his disciples and his followers today:

- Embodying the Divine vocation in practical ministry.
- Creating and building up a community committed to it.
- Hailing its presence within people and society.
- Developing disciplines and spiritualities to support it.
- Dealing with its detractors and opponents.

In practice, not every one of these elements takes place in any one situational happening. But if all of the elements are not coherent with the total Project, then something is missing. At the end of a UTU Institute on Bible and Practice, I concluded:

> We recreate the Gospel in our own time by repeating bits of the actions of the Gospels in our own contexts. We need the variety of Gospel stories to discover which stories we are being called upon to re-enact, but also which contexts, problems, issues, people and communities these stories belong to. (Vincent in Vincent and Rowland, 2001: 108)

So, our search for God's Project leads us to search in the city, with questions like:

- Who really needs this story?
- Who has things going on that only make sense in the light of this story?
- Who has happenings which seem most naturally able to utilize the words of this story?
- Where do there seem to be actions and practice that are coherent with the actions and practice described in this story?
- Where are people using this story for solidarity, strengthening and projection. (Vincent in Rowland and Vincent, 2001: 107–08)

BIBLIOGRAPHY

Albertz, R. 1994. *A History of Israelite Religion in the Old Testament Period*. London: SCM Press.

Alexander, L. (Ed.). 1991. *Images of Empire*. Sheffield: JSOT Press.

Alexander, L. 2006. *Acts in its Ancient Literary Context*. London: T. & T. Clark.

Archbishop's Commission on Urban Priority Areas. 1985. *Faith in the City: A Call for Action by Church and Nation*. London: Church House Publishing.

Ashton, J. 1991. *Understanding the Fourth Gospel*. Oxford: Oxford University Press.

Balch, D. L. and C. Osiek (Eds). 2003. *Early Christian Families in Context: An Interdisciplinary Dialogue*. Grand Rapids, MI/Cambridge: Eerdmans.

Barton, S. C. 1992. *The Spirituality of the Gospels*. London: SPCK.

Batey, R. A. 1991. *Jesus and the Forgotten City: New Light on Sepphoris and the Urban World of Jesus*. Grand Rapids, MI: Baker.

Bauckham, R. (Ed.). 1998. *The Gospels for All Christians: Re-thinking the Gospel Audiences*. Edinburgh: T. & T. Clark.

Blasi, A. J., J. Duhaime and P.-A. Turcotte. 2002. *Handbook of Early Christianity: Social Science Approaches*.Walnut Creek, CA/Oxford: Alta Mira Press.

Browning, I. 1982. *Jerash and Decapolis*. London: Chatto & Windus.

Brueggemann, W. 1997. *Theology of the Old Testament: Testimony, Dispute, Advocacy*. Minneapolis, MN: Fortress Press.

Burridge, R. 2007. *Imitating Jesus: An Inclusive Approach to New Testament Ethics*. Grand Rapids, MI/Cambridge: Eerdmans.

Carter, W. 2004. *Matthew and the Margins*. London/New York: T. & T. Clark International.

Cassidy, R. J. 1978. *Jesus, Politics and Society: A Study of Luke's Gospel*. Maryknoll, NY: Orbis Books.

Coogan, M. D. (Ed.). 1998. *Oxford History of the Biblical World*. Oxford: Oxford University Press.

Commission on Urban Life. 2006. *Faithful Cities: A Call for Celebration, Vision and Justice*. London: Church House Publishing/Methodist Publishing House.

Crossan, J. D. 1998. *The Birth of Christianity*. Edinburgh: T. & T. Clark.

_____ 2007. *God and Empire: Jesus Against Rome, Then and Now*. New York/San Francisco: Harper.

Crossan, J. D. and J. L. Reed. 2001. *Excavating Jesus: Beneath the Stories, Behind the Texts*. London: SPCK.

_____ 2005. *In Search of Paul: How Jesus' Apostle Opposed Rome's Empire with God's Kingdom*. London: SPCK.

Davies, W. D. 1974. *The Gospel and the Land: Early Christianity and Jewish Territorial Doctrine*. Berkley, CA: University of California Press.

Davey, A. 2001. *Urban Christianity and Global Order*. London: SPCK.

Downing, G. 1987. *Jesus and the Threat of Freedom*. London: SCM Press.

Duffield, I. and R. Pagan. 2008. *Jesus' Radical Resistance*. Sheffield: Urban Theology Unit.

Dunn, J. D. G. 1998. *The Theology of Paul the Apostle*. Grand Rapids, MI: Eerdmans.

_____ 2003. *Jesus Remembered*. Grand Rapids, MI: Eerdmans.

Foster, P. 2004. *Community, Law and Mission in Matthew's Gospel*. Tübingen: Mohr Siebeck.

Freyne, S. 2004. *Jesus, a Jewish Galilean*. London/New York: T. & T. Clark International.

Freyne, S. 2008. "Galilee, Jesus and the Contribution of Archaeology", *Expository Times*, 119 (12), 573–81.

Green, L. 2001. *The Impact of the Global: An Urban Theology*. Sheffield: Urban Theology Unit.

_____ 2003. *Urban Ministry and the Kingdom of God*. London: SPCK.

Hammond, N. G. L. 1980. *Alexander the Great: King, Commander and Statesman*. Park Ridge, NJ: Noyes.

Harding, M. (Ed.). 2003. *Early Christian Life and Thought in Social Context: A Reader*. London/New York: T. & T. Clark International.

Harris, G. 2004. *Mission in the Gospels*. Peterborough: Epworth Press.

Harrison, R. K. (Ed.). 1985. *Major Cities of the Biblical World*. Nashville, TE: Thomas Nelson.

Harvey, A. E. 1990. *Strenuous Demands: The Ethic of Jesus*. London: SCM Press.

Herzog, W. R. 1994. *Parables as Subversive Speech: Jesus as Pedagogue of the Oppressed*. Louisville, KY: Westminster John Knox Press.

_____ 2000. *Jesus, Justice and the Reign of God*. Louisville, KY: Westminster John Knox Press.

_____ 2004. *Prophet and Teacher*. Louisville, KY: Westminster John Knox Press.

Hill, J. V. (Ed.). 1998. *Common Life in the Early Church*. Harrisburg, PA: Trinity Press International.

Holgate, D. A. and R. Starr. 2006. *SCM Study Guide to Biblical Hermeneutics*. London: SCM Press.

Holland, J. and P. Henriot. 1983. *Social Analysis: Linking Faith and Justice* (revised edn). Maryknoll, NY: Orbis Books.

Hook, R. F. 1980. *The Social Context of Paul's Ministry: Tentmaking and Apostleship*. Philadelphia, PA: Fortress Press.

Horrell, D. G. 1996. *The Social Ethos of the Corinthian Correspondence*. Edinburgh: T. & T. Clark.

Horsley, R. A. 1995. *Galilee: History, Politics, People*. Valley Forge, PA: Trinity Press International.

_____ (Ed.). 2000. *Paul and Politics*. Harrisburg, PA: Trinity Press International.

_____ 2003. *Jesus and Empire: The Kingdom of God and the New World Disorder*. Minneapolis, MI: Fortress Press.

Howard-Brook, W. 1994. *Becoming Children of God: John's Gospel and Radical Discipleship*. Maryknoll, NY: Orbis Books.

Howard-Brook, W. and S. Ringe (Eds). 2002. *The New Testament – Introducing the Way of Discipleship*. Maryknoll, NY: Orbis Books.

Inge, J. 2003. *A Christian Theology of Place*. Aldershot: Ashgate.

Josephus. 1981. *The Jewish War* (tr. G. A. Williamson). Harmondsworth: Penguin Books.

Lane Fox, R. 1987. *Pagans and Christians*. New York: Knopf.

Lieu, J. M. 1998. "The 'Attraction of Women' in Early Judeism", *Journal for the Study of the New Testament*, 72, 16–19.

Luz, U. 1994. *Matthew in History: Interpretation, Influence and Effects*. Minneapolis, MI: Fortress Press.

Malina, B. J. 2001. *The Social Gospel of Jesus*. Minneapolis, MN: Fortress Press.

McLennan, J. S. 1991. *Power and Politics in Palestine, 100BC–70AD*. Sheffield: JSOT.

Meeks, W. A. 1983. *The First Urban Christians: The Social World of the Apostle Paul*. New Haven, CT: Yale University Press.

Meggitt, J. J. 1998. *Paul, Poverty and Survival*. Edinburgh: T. & T. Clark.

Methodist Church. 1997. *The Cities: A Methodist Report*. London: Methodist Church & NCH Action for Children.

Miller, S. 2004. *Women in Mark's Gospel*. London/New York: T. & T. Clark International.

Moxnes, H. 2003. *Putting Jesus in his Place: A Radical View of Household and Kingdom*. Louisville, KY/London: Westminster John Knox Press.

Myers, C. 1988. *Binding the Strong Man*. Maryknoll, NY: Orbis Books.

Pomeroy, S. 1995. *Goddesses, Whores, Wives and Slaves*. New York: Schoken.

Prior, M. 1995. *Jesus the Liberator*. Sheffield: Academic Press.

Reed, J. L. 2000. *Archaeology and the Galilean Jesus*. Harrisburg, PA: Trinity Press International.

Rowland, C. and J. Vincent (Eds). 2001. *Bible and Practice*. Sheffield: Urban Theology Unit.

Sandercock, L. 2003. *Cosmopolis II: Mongrel Cities of the 21st Century*. London/New York: Continuum.

Sawicki, M. 2000. *Crossing Galilee: Architectures of Contact in the Occupied Land of Jesus*. Harrisburg, PA: Trinity Press International.

Schüssler Fiorenza, E. 1983. *In Memory of Her: A Feminist Theological Reconstruction of Christian Origins*. London: SCM Press.

Segovia, F. (Ed.). 1985. *Discipleship in the New Testament*. Philadelphia, PA: Fortress Press.

Smith, D. E. 2003. *From Symposium to Eucharist: The Banquet in the Early Christian World*. Minneapolis, MN: Fortress Press.

Spencer, F. S. 2004. *Dancing Girls, Loose Ladies and Women of the Cloth*. New York/London: Continuum.

Sperber, D. 1998. *The City in Roman Palestine*. New York/Oxford: Oxford University Press.

Stegemann, E. W. and W. Stegemann. 1999. *The Jesus Movement: A Social History of its First Century*. Edinburgh: T. & T. Clark.

Taylor, V. 1952. *The Gospel According to St. Mark*. London: Macmillan.

Thiede, C. P. 2004. *The Cosmopolitan World of Jesus*. London: SPCK.

Theissen, G. 1978. *The First Followers of Jesus*. London: SCM Press.

_____ 1982. *The Social Setting of Pauline Christianity: Essays on Corinth.* Edinburgh : T. & T. Clark.

Vincent, J. (Ed.). 2003. *Faithfulness in the City.* Hawarden: Monad Press.

_____ 2004. *Radical Jesus: The Way of Jesus Then and Now* (2nd Edn). Sheffield: Ashram Press.

_____ 2005. *Outworkings: Gospel Practice and Interpretation.* Sheffield: Urban Theology Unit.

_____ (Ed.) 2006. *Mark: Gospel of Action; Personal and Community Responses.* London: SPCK.

_____ 2008. "Outworkings: Twelve as Christian Community". *Expository Times,* 119 (12), 582–88.

_____ 2009. *Theology from the City.* Forthcoming.

Volf, M. 1996. *Exclusion and Embrace: Theological Reflections on Identity, Otherness and Reconciliation.* Nashville, TE: Abingdon.

Volf, M. and D. C. Bass. 2002. *Practicing Theology: Beliefs and Practices in Christian Life.* Grand Rapids, MI: Eerdmans.

Wengst, K. 1987. *Pax Romana and the Peace of Jesus Christ.* London: SCM Press.

Wilde, W. 2006. *Crossing the River of Fire.* Peterborough: Epworth Press.

Winter, B. W. 2001. *After Paul Left Corinth: The Influence of Secular and Social Change.* Grand Rapids, MI/Cambridge: William B. Eerdmans.

Index

Index of Biblical References

AUTHOR INDEX

Subject Index

...nigsville, PA USA
...ovember 2010

9519BV00003B/54/P

SUBJECT INDEX

249519BV00003B/54/P

Breinigsville, PA USA
17 November 2010